P. J. Cratty has spent almost 44 years in the newspaper business at 13 separate community publications in six different states. He has served in every capacity possible in newsrooms – as an obit writer; sportswriter; sports editor; school, police, city, county, and state beats, as well as a columnist, investigative reporter; and as a city, copydesk, managing, and executive editor. His experience includes stints as both a weekly editor and general manager of a weekly chain and work at dailies ranging in circulation from 5,000 to 40,000.

D1423700

To Kath, who, despite how everything turned out, was the best decision she and I ever made. She gave me two wonderful daughters, who, along with her, were the bedrock of my career herein contained. Then she was left to raise them on her own. It was a chore that nobody but her could have accomplished and one that allowed me to selfishly follow my own life's adventure recounted in this book. I know it doesn't come close to an even trade, but certainly you got the best part of the bargain.

P. J. Cratty

(30)

FROM WOODWARD AND BERNSTEIN TO DONALD TRUMP: A CAREER

AUSTIN MACAULEY PUBLISHERS™

LONDON · CAMBRIDGE · NEW YORK · SHARJAH

Ordering Information:
Quantity sales: special discounts are available on quantity purchases by corporations, associations, and others. For details, contact the publisher at the address below.

Publisher's Cataloging-in-Publication data
Cratty, P. J.
(30)
From Woodward and Bernstein to Donald Trump: A Career

ISBN 9781641829748 (Paperback)
ISBN 9781641829755 (Hardback)
ISBN 9781645366560 (ePub e-book)

Library of Congress Control Number: 2019920016

www.austinmacauley.com/us

First Published (2020)
Austin Macauley Publishers LLC
40 Wall Street, 28th Floor
New York, NY 10005
USA
mail-usa@austinmacauley.com
+1 (646) 5125767

There are many people I need to acknowledge for my 44-year career in the newspaper business, and perhaps I should start from the beginning.

To the late Delbert Roberts, who took a fresh-out-of-college rookie with little to no typing skills and broke him in. To Darrell Bates – also no longer with us – who took a rookie sportswriter and carried him at his first major paper. Then there was Dave Elbert, who is probably most responsible for the newspaperman I became. The late great Forrest Kilmer, who, like myself, was a former paratrooper who no doubt protected my job security, considering all the trouble I caused him.

The Hurt brothers, Murray and Nolan – fellow hometown scribes and family friends – who made me into the columnist I later became. Murray was the greatest columnist I ever knew. My favorite publisher, and that's saying quite a bit because I liked only one other, my wife, Scott Champion. Rich Heiland and Dave Berry put up with a lot of my shit but have remained close friends ever since my Texas days. And I shouldn't neglect Dave Hawk.

And also, every colleague I met, worked with and for, and/or mentored along the way. They are too numerous to catalog but I can't remember too many I couldn't at least be in the same newsroom with. I'm sure that many of them couldn't say the same about me. But at least I'm sure that I'll always be remembered.

1. Bad Dreams

"Shit," he said just above a whisper as he sat straight up in bed, soaked in sweat, almost as if he'd been struck by lightning.

It was 3:00 a.m. by the green glow of the digital clock on the VCR on top of the television across his cluttered one-room plus a bath. In the distance, he could hear a train whistle, as the South Shore rolled into Indiana City, Mich., from the east, looking for takers headed to downtown Chicago, as it was every couple of hours.

Another day was beginning for the rest of the world, but not him. He still had another 12 hours or so to kill before starting the second shift on the copy desk at The Courier in 1998.

Once again, he had the uncontrollable urge to take a piss, and since he was already wide awake thanks to the same dream that seemed to interrupt some of his sleeping moments the past few years, he went ahead and stumbled in the dark to the bathroom. He cussed every time his foot landed on a stray shoe, plastic fork, paper plate or some other unknown object.

It wasn't that his apartment, situated on the upper story of a modest red-brick home about 10 blocks from the lake, was that big, but he always had a pile of junk lying on the floor and the journey across the space was not unlike a walk through a minefield in the dark. And God knows he was never one for bright lights in the middle of the night. He was always worried about his night vision, which he was just certain was compromised by lights. It was either that or his inability to fall asleep with the lights on.

As he stood pissing in the darkness, which was broken only by the lights along 11th Street streaming in through the slatted rollout window at the south end of the room, he couldn't get that dream out of his head. But then he never could.

It always started the same way. Or at least the part of it he could recall later seemed to begin the same. Like most of his nocturnal journeys, there were parts that were as clear as a bell and parts that seemed to float through the air, nameless, faceless, and placeless.

Three soldiers, their jungle fatigues, drenched with sweat, are standing on a dirt road that forms one wall of a half-dried rice paddy on a cloudless Southeast Asian day. The sun is so bright, the trio is forced to squint, and one of them puts his hand up in the air in a vain attempt to cut the almost painful rays.

None of them say a word as they consider the questioning eyes of an old man, who looks as dried and worn as the field behind him. The shriveled Gook stands in front of them with a look on his face suspended somewhere between a fake smile and absolute terror.

One of the young soldiers reaches into his deep fatigue pockets and, with tears in his eyes, hands the old man every scrap of Piasters he has on him.

For years, that was all Cratty could ever conjure up in the way of a wartime memory. It was always at about that same moment in this recurring movie of the mind – or was it a nightmare? – that he'd awaken, sometimes quietly, sometimes in a cold sweat with an audible cry, like tonight…or better yet, this morning.

His own private dream was rather tame by comparison to some he'd heard of. And it hadn't even crossed into his dreams until sometime in the 1980s, a good 20 years after his tour of duty with the 1st Brigade of the 101st had ended.

Before that, it was an all too clear memory of one afternoon in that tour.

He knew that one of the soldiers in his dream, the one with tears in his eyes, was himself, and he had absolutely no idea who the others were. He knew it was him, but it was one of those things that's peculiar about dreams. You recognize the characters without really seeming to use your sense of sight.

It was almost his only lingering memory from Viet Nam. It and an even stranger remembrance about an old woman standing naked beside Highway 1 and shouting unintelligible epithets in Vietnamese as his outfit passed were the only things remotely resembling nightmares, he retained from his stint on the other side of the Pacific in the mid-1960s. He had been 10,000 miles from his Midwestern roots and an entire universe away from the 18 years of his life before Viet Nam and more than three decades since.

It wasn't as if he had found anything like home since leaving the small-town Midwest. He'd spent the 30 plus years since 'Nam moving from one newspaper job to another in what was quickly becoming a futile attempt at finding a stable work environment. His two grown daughters were always distant voices on the telephone as he moved from paper to paper, trying to find someplace to land and at least build something remotely resembling retirement security.

His connection with his two daughters was probably the closest thing to an anchor in his journeyman's life spent at 13 publications in six different states by the time it ended.

However, that quest for any real retirement security was also quickly becoming a pipe dream. He hadn't spent much more than a couple of years at six or seven of the rags he'd bounced around in just the past quarter century. Just like his three marriages, only one of which – his first, gave him his two daughters – he'd spent more than a couple of years in.

Other than those two dreams, which he never discussed with anybody else until early in the 1990s and then only in counseling sessions, his recollections of the Viet Nam War were quite uneventful, or at least he thought so.

Oh, there were flashes, bits and pieces of other things that darted in and out of his memory about that time. But there were surprisingly few faces and only portions of names, almost exclusively last names. There was also very little in the way of fear drawn back to the surface by his wartime memories.

That was one of the things he just couldn't seem to conjure up from that time: fear. He certainly remembered what fear felt like and even smelled like. And he was revisited by that memory from time to time, that immediate hot flash and deep ache in the stomach. He just couldn't quite remember those times, save for one or two, he'd felt that way in 'Nam. And perhaps that was one of the greatest benefits garnered from his 12 months over there: He could honestly say he hadn't been truly afraid of anything else ever since.

But there must have been times when he was white-knuckle scared overseas. He just couldn't reproduce but a couple of the names, faces, or facts.

Those two recurring dreams came the closest to that memory of fear. The first, he understood only too well, the other, he could not and never would. That shriveled old lady was like his own private Fellini film, full of what he was sure was twisted symbolism and in a tongue he couldn't understand.

"So, who's got the Thousand Island?" said Cratty as he started slicing a tomato to place on his usual vegetable sandwich. His outfit used to stop at roadside stands along Highway 1 that ran up the Vietnamese coast and purchase the makings – a head of lettuce, a few tomatoes, an onion or two, and a loaf of fresh French bread.

The Vietnamese could make some amazing French bread.

But the recipe needed a generous helping of Thousand Island to make it palatable for the many American G.I.'s who used to enjoy the treat.

Cratty had acquired quite a taste for French bread during his stint overseas. But try as he might, the variety in the States never seemed to match up with the taste he remembered across the pond.

"Cratty, what in the hell do you and DeBonis think you're doing?" barked Sgt. Davis, his squat-built squad leader.

"Just havin' a sandwich, Sarge," replied DeBonis, not giving Cratty, who already had a mouthful, a chance to answer.

Then it hit. The loudest noise he'd ever heard, just like an M-80 had gone off inside his head. A flash of white-hot light and a seeming dust storm almost knocked him off the wheel well of the jeep.

Davis, who seemed to be knocked to the ground by the sound, screamed, "Incoming!" as he laid belly down beside the roadway. The Recon Platoon, providing security for convoys of deuce and a halves ferrying between Cam Ranh Bay – where the unit had come ashore just a few short weeks earlier – and Nha Trang – some 35 miles north along the South China Sea – had come under enemy fire for one of the first times during its tour of duty.

He certainly remembered what fear felt like that day. A lone mortar round fell to earth 100 yards from Highway 1 and it was like the end of the world.

There wasn't a day that passed since that he wasn't mindful of his 12-month stint in Viet Nam. It wasn't unlike his knowing that he was born and raised in a small farming and railroad community, had a mother, father, brother, a sister and later a couple of kids. And yet it was even more than that. It was something he never spent a single 24-hour period since without remembering.

But none of the remembrances, which seemed to float just below the surface, were anything he'd call real nightmares. Nothing that brought back the fear he knew instinctively that he must have felt.

And there were plenty of days he never remembered his father, mother, or most of the rest of his family, save his two daughters. But he was sure of one thing: He was Cratty, Patrick J., Recon (Hawk) Platoon, Headquarters & Headquarters Company, 2/327, 1st Brigade, 101st Airborne Division.

He could rattle off the words and numbers just like he'd been hypnotized and the one in control of the parlor trick had clapped their hands. It was just that automatic.

Every single day since that hot, early July morning in 1966 when he stepped off a plane in California returning from overseas, he knew that he'd been there. And now, 30 years later, the memory – although less exact and coming in spurts and jolts – was no less intense. He knew he would spend the rest of his natural life as a Viet Nam veteran and little else. It would be a constant part of his psychological make-up, character or anything else that makes one human being different from another.

There might be times he couldn't tell you where he was or even why, but he could always remember that Viet Nam made him different, quite a bit different from almost every other person in the world.

It was a lot like the day he suddenly noticed that the name for the country that lies along the east coast of Southeast Asia had been compacted into just one word. He'd once come across a poster of a Viet Nam vet, noting that for those who were there, it will always be VIET NAM.

He wasn't quite sure just when the switch in grammar came into use, but it was a convention of speech he would almost religiously try to avoid.

His memories of 'Nam and the fact that he was a veteran of the conflict just seemed to hang in the air every day. He would be out running and in the most unimaginable

15

situations and/or circumstances and he'd see himself as a Viet Nam vet, different from almost everyone else he'd come across day-to-day, week-to-week, month-to-month, or year-to-year for some 30 trips around the Sun now.

That was perhaps the most constant feeling he had associated with Viet Nam, a distinct knowledge that he was indeed different. He saw himself as separate, apart from the rest of society. He was a Viet Nam veteran, and just about everybody else he had reason to deal with every single day – from the newsroom to the street – was not.

He'd hear that distinct eggbeater like sound of a helicopter blade churning up the air someplace in the distance, and he'd instantly be back in 'Nam.

"Goddamned choppers," he once said. "I'll bet I never get that womp, womp, womp out of my ears."

Well, so far, he was riding a sure thing.

"I wonder if they can tell," he'd say to himself sometimes. "I wonder if they know that I was in 'Nam. Do I look different? Is it…" or a million other mental inquiries of more or less importance.

Of course, they could tell. He'd made every effort to make sure they could, from the baseball cap he wore adorned with jump wings, CIB and 101st Screaming Eagle, to that gruff exterior he'd meticulously crafted for himself warning everybody else to stand clear.

He so liked the image of the "could go off the edge at any moment" persona he had perfected. From the hat on his head to the ponytail, Cratty was the picture of an anti-social misfit. And he didn't give a good goddamn who knew it.

It was probably just that unassailable stature that led to his string of failed matrimonial arrangements and his constant search for a new job.

Cratty did not fit in for too long anywhere. There would always come a breaking point – his mostly. He'd eventually get around to taking the roof off the building and exit while the debris and dust were settling.

Hell, once he'd charged out so fucking fast, he had to ask an ex-colleague to look through the contents of his former desk in case he'd left something of value behind.

Of course, this character trait also attracted some small bit of respect, especially from the younger members of the staff. Well, at least, that's the way it always seemed early on. As he got older, and the newsroom staffers got younger, the generation gap was getting wider and wider by the minute.

He laid back down in the dark and tried desperately to get back to sleep. But it was no use. He rolled from side to side and tried his best to get comfortable, a feat he could seldom accomplish on a good night, let alone following one of those dreams.

He hadn't really slept all that well ever since returning from overseas. The glorious war stories about GIs sleeping with one eye open, although popular among war movie buffs, was never something Cratty could accomplish. So, he was a habitual light sleeper, which is the same as saying he'd find himself waking up every few minutes and staring at a clock.

Come to think of it, Cratty would spend each and every night of the rest of his life getting little more than a couple of hours' sleep.

Minutes stretched into an hour, and one strung out into three. It seemed like he couldn't help but stare at the green glowing time on top of the TV every five minutes. Then the sun was up, and he found himself staring at the ceiling.

The first ring was mistaken for part of another half-dream, but by the third, he'd scrambled for the phone, which like almost everything else in the cracker box he lived in was buried under some dirty running gear.

It was the office asking if he could come in an hour or so early for a meeting.

The VCR was showing 8:00, so he had managed to fall back to sleep after all. But it must have been a very light imitation, because unlike the 3:00 a.m. alert, he could recall nothing in the way of a dream.

That meant he still had at least six hours to kill before what was probably another in a long line of meaningless newsroom gatherings. He knew it was useless to try and go back to sleep, so he opted for an early run.

During the workout, he never considered the reason for the early phone call, but it did manage to annoy him just a bit.

He liked newsroom meetings of any kind about as much as he liked the white shirt, bright-tied management types who called them. It was always one of the same two things on the agenda, some "amazing subscription promotion" or the latest hair up the ass of a publisher or a publisher wannabe who wasn't fit to empty the wastebaskets in the newsroom let alone actually run one.

The Courier had a new publisher there because the publication had just been purchased by a new group, which in this business usually means a raft of seemingly ridiculous changes, stupid suggestions, and the usual dumbass questions about "just what do you do here?"

He was officially on The Courier copy desk in Michigan, but he was also its most controversial – as well as best-read – columnist. He had landed himself in the center of yet another Category 5 journalistic hurricane exactly where he always wanted to be.

Cratty was one of those newspaper hacks that always seemed to find the usually untold seam in a story that inevitably led to uncovering what some would just as soon not know. Call it a knack or a talent, but the columnist always seemed to be at the center of one storm or another.

Recently, he'd been leaning quite heavily on the local Democrat establishment, which was solidly in control of things in Indiana City but was undergoing something of a civil war, as at least two factions fought for outright control.

Following one of Cratty's recent offerings, those in charge at City Hall were reeling after the mayor was exposed as feathering his own nest at the expense of the citizenry. And, as sure as clockwork, the Democrats not in charge of City Hall were celebrating.

One of the outside party's guiding lights picked up the phone to congratulate the opinion writer.

Now, those particular calls, as predictable and fawning as they usually were, were somewhat uncomfortable from Cratty's point of view. It always occurred to him that his epistles belonged to him and no one else, no matter what those on either side of the subject might think.

And if Cratty was nothing else, he was certainly an equal opportunity assailant. It was his version of the old saw "What goes around, comes around."

Upon the latest congratulatory call, Cratty was quick to blunt the praise with a warning.

"Now it's not that I don't appreciate laudatory comments on my work, but I don't want you to get the wrong idea. I would appreciate that you remember this call when the GUN is pointed in your direction," Cratty reported, pouring more than just a bit of icy water on the festivities.

"Because sure as hell that day will come and somebody else will be making this celebratory connection."

"And I promise you, I'll tell them the same thing I'm telling you now when that call comes."

The new boss was what's known in the business as a "slash and burn artist" – a guy who's hired on contract to come into a newly purchased paper and cut everything down to the bolts in the floor to build up the bottom line.

The purpose is either to pull the entire operation back from the brink of bankruptcy, trim it down as for a perceived new market, or simply to puff up the profit margin to look good for another new buyer, who is usually waiting in the wings when the current purchaser discovers just how much of a hit he'll take repaying the added debt that accumulates once you make such a purchase.

It's the multimillion-dollar version of buyer's remorse.

And anymore in publishing that was a common malady. One newspaper chain looking to grow its revenue opportunities meets another looking to get itself out of the debt it assumed by doing the exact same thing.

The business model, such as it is, dictates that the only way to stay ahead of the curve and bankruptcy was to gobble up as many publications which for the front office types is equated with growth and thereby profit.

Of course, it's a never-ending chase for ever-expanding properties they can never properly manage and the need to instantly cut everything to the bone, which usually means less investment in both equipment and people.

Then the bright idea to reduce the need for staff by combining critical operations, such as copy desks, printing presses and bookkeeping.

The news can then be gathered by a skeleton staff and the pages can be designed and put together at an entirely different spot and pressed at still another.

This greatly reduces the local connection to subscribers, who are being targeted by centralized functions often hundreds of miles if not more apart and certainly with no knowledge or feeling for the location that originated the news in the first place.

Podunk, wherever, is just a name on the masthead, printed by someone who could care less and probably couldn't even find the spot on a map.

But, that's the wave of the future in the business, where increasing debt load and pushing local operations to the limit of endurance and resources makes for a better return on somebody's investment.

The Courier was originally owned by a family. But like a lot of family-owned publications in the business, not every succeeding generation has the same passion for newspapers.

And since the love of the art is one of those essential ingredients necessary for survival, the urge to sell-out, grab a quick profit, and then move on usually overcomes the idea of a legacy.

That usually leads to cut-rate prices and investment groups picking at the carcass.

When the buyout came at Indiana City, Cratty tried reaching out to some of his connections, who might be able to provide some information on the new owner.

What neither he nor the connection knew, was that the purchasing chain had undergone a couple of buyouts itself and was not even a poor imitation of its former self.

Unfortunately, Cratty had already assured his colleagues that the new buyers were OK and could be trusted to not feed on The Courier like vultures. That was a mistake he would feel bad about for years after. It also made him warry of such situations from that day in the mid-1990s until he gave up the business two decades later.

2. Battling Machines

"I'll be go'ta hell. Goddamnit!" he practically screamed across the newsroom.

"This fuckin' computer is a bigger pain in the ass than it's worth."

But even as he said it, while the screen flashed that frustrating green and useless message: 'This application has unexpectedly quit due to an error of type 2,' he knew it was a gross exaggeration.

Cratty knew that the computer age hadn't come a minute too soon for the newspaper business, that profession he'd spent almost every second of his working life trying to perfect over the previous 25 plus years.

And he'd probably spend the remainder of that life trying his damnedest to cope with these goddamned contrary monstrosities in an attempt to get it right.

Hell, he'd more than likely have a fatal stroke about two-thirds of the way through a column someday and expire in the saddle. That was the thought he toyed with probably a little more than he should have.

But for the moment, at least, he'd have to wait to either die or continue that quest, as the machine made that characteristic musical tone that denotes a crash.

Briefly, he thought back to his beginnings in the business, back to the spring of 1971, fresh out of college and barely able to find the right keys on the typewriter. In fact, he had no idea where any of the keys were on the old Smith/Corona he found himself behind that first day at the old LaMotte Recorder, a quarter century before.

He finally found the county coroner and sheriff exchanging war stories in the basement of a funeral home as they almost jokingly cleaned out the contents of one of the two body bags that lay on the table between them.

"Remember that time it took us three months to find that guy who wandered away from the county nursing home?" asked the coroner.

"Yup, he'd curled up and died and was buried in the snow," was the answer. "Hell, we didn't find him till the snow melted sometime the following spring."

"Yeah, most of the parts were coming off in our hands as we tried to pick 'em up, as I remember it."

It was cub reporter Cratty's first hot news assignment. Some guy had shot-gunned his estranged wife and then himself on a small farm just outside of Bushing, a town northeast of LaMotte.

He'd been sent out to run down either the county sheriff or coroner to put together a story for that afternoon's edition. After driving to the scene, he'd been told that both county officials had taken the two bodies, or at least what was left of them, to the funeral home back in LaMotte, which was also the coroner's place of business.

It was almost a 30-mile round trip, and by the time he found the two of them laughing their way through the gruesome task at hand, he was only three blocks from the newspaper office where he'd started an hour and a half earlier.

The look on the two petty politicians' faces and their near jovial approach to the tragedy had started a slow burn inside of him. Perhaps it was that incident which pointed him in the direction of poking such nasty fun at these kinds of individuals in his columns later in his career.

It was something that would stick with him throughout the years he spent in the profession, which turned out to be four decades.

He hadn't even learned to type until his very last quarter at school and didn't even know that he wanted to work at a newspaper until just before he finished his education.

"They simply called me one day," he used to say of his exit from State University in LaMotte, "and told me I had enough hours and they'd appreciate it if I'd put in for graduation."

He was already a pain in the ass back then, always wanting to be at the center of the universe, no matter where or what that universe was.

He'd joined with a group of students to help start an off-campus publication as a junior at State. But unlike the vast majority of the other off-campus, unrecognized sheets of the time – the late 1960s – his newspaper was more reactionary than revolutionary, forming as a counter to the on-campus publication that had been taken over by the school's leftist fringe.

Cratty even had to be out of step way back then. While most of the rest of the youth of America were taking to the streets to protest the war in Viet Nam, a war he'd served a year in before coming home and going to college, he was bound and determined to lead a parade in the exact opposite direction. While young people around the world were trying to start the blaze that would become the counterculture, Cratty practically saw himself as the single-handed counterrevolution to that culture, trying to piss out their match before it reached the kindling.

But that was not the case these days.

Hopefully, he hadn't lost the nearly 20 inches of copy he'd already completed toward Thursday's column instalment in the most recent crash. But even that, he knew, wouldn't have been a complete disaster.

Oh, he'd have still wasted the better part of the previous hour toying with the grain of a thought he always seemed able to eventually turn into a twice-weekly column, but he'd take it like he took most such setbacks: It must be a sign that the original version just wasn't good enough anyway.

And, to his way of thinking, it probably wasn't.

But, like so many other opinions he espoused in the '90s and after, this was one he'd made a complete reversal on.

"Quick, get a typewriter and start copying down everything on the VDT (Video Display Terminal of an earlier age)!" yelled somebody from the other end of the newsroom.

"This thing is starting to flicker," announced another.

"Shit on a stick, we're gonna crash!" cried somebody else.

In those days, it was not uncommon to have the entire system – one of the first in the newspaper business in the early 1970s – crash (shut down) five or six times a day. And that was before you could save your copy and then pick up where you left off once the machines were back up and running.

Cratty recalled those early days of computers in journalism with no small amount of terror.

"Ya' know, if they could invent one of these damn things to cover a basketball game and didn't have to actually talk with it, they'd drop all of us like a bad habit," Cratty said disparagingly about the devices.

His first sports editor, Gerry "J.J." Juergens, refused to even sit in front of a VDT. He'd type his stories and columns on an old manual at home and then force one of the rookies, like Cratty at that time, to put it into the system between all of his other chores.

But thinking back to those days when he used to have to lug a 30-pound electric typewriter, a ream of paper, 35 pounds more of telecopier – a contraption that was as unreliable as it was cumbersome – up six flights of stairs to the press box at the old University of Iowa Fieldhouse just to cover a single basketball game, Cratty was more than willing to admit that the computer age represented progress.

He would later write a poem about those early days of computers. In fact, throughout his career, he'd often resort to sarcastic rhyming missives about the things that tripped his somewhat twisted sense of newsroom humor.

A rookie it's been said was once lying stone dead,
somewhere on a cluttered newsroom floor.
As he struck on a key of his new VDT
a green flash jumped up to implore.
"It appears, my good man, there's now nothing you can
do to retrieve what you just wrote.

27

So, the answer it seems after all of the screams
is take a copy knife to your own throat."
He EN'd to end it and SE'd to send it.
And send it he wished that he could.
All his masterful type throughout the long night,
was now locked inside it for GOOD!

And the tales did make for some great "in my day" stories. But all in all, the computer age had made life much easier for journalists.

It also nearly cost some of the early so-called computer experts their lives in more than one newsroom.

Cratty came close to sending one to microchip heaven back in the early 1970s.

He was just putting the wraps on a 30-inch piece he had slaved over for the better part of a week. It was an in-depth item about the storied prep basketball tradition in his hometown, where the school board was trying to swing a multimillion-dollar bond referendum by threatening to discontinue the high school's athletic program.

Of course, it was all a crock of shit, and Cratty had an anonymous source in the schools' administration who was feeding him the real facts and figures.

He was on the last sentence of the thing when the screen flashed brighter and then went blank.

Just then, a computer whiz from the company that had sold the piece of shit system chimed in. Like most of the rest of those sent to nursemaid the newfangled devices, he didn't have the first clue about the newspaper business. He came waltzing down the tunnel from the back shop and, with a big shit-eating grin on his face, announced, "We're in a crash."

Cratty immediately went for the guy, plowing all the way from the sports department across the newsroom with his arms outstretched and his hands already forming a chokehold. If two guys on the state desk hadn't tackled and then sat on top of him, Cratty quite probably would have wound up in jail on an attempted murder rap, or worse.

Then, just when it seemed things had cooled down, the computer shit-stain cracks wise with "Well, what's he so upset about? He can write it again, can't he?"

Cratty had already tossed the two state desk employees off and was dashing across the newsroom again. This time, he had one of those three-foot tall circular, metal trash cans extended high over his head, intent on making the guy a set of oversized braces.

But nowadays, he thought nothing of sitting down and writing a column again. However, there were no longer many crashes like those experienced in the '70s, so it was a little easier restructuring a column when you had something to work with.

Cratty had developed quite a following over the previous eight or nine years since returning from Texas and shifting over to hard news in the early '90s. He had an ever-growing list of enemies cultivated with pieces that were often explosive, at the very least caustic and never dull.

Politicians beware: Somebody always finds out

Ya know, I've been in this business going on 26 years now, and I never cease to be amazed by the, well for the lack of a better term, stupidity of some people.

What makes usually regular, levelheaded and basically honest Americans, those most generally in elective and/or appointed positions of responsibility, believe that 'NO ONE WILL EVER FIND OUT'?

No matter where I go, and I've been a lot of places in two and half decades, I always run into some self-satisfied stiff who's just convinced that he/she invented the political talent for lying.

Let me preface this next bit of advice with a rule that's been gathered from my vast experience in this industry.

THERE IS NO SUCH THING AS A SECRET. By its very nature, a SECRET is something that just one person knows. When more than one person knows, it is no longer a secret. And something that is buried deep in the mind of just one person is not a 'secret,' it is little more than a fantasy!

When two people know said 'secret' then you can bet the ranch on the fact that four, eight and God knows how many others are aware of the basic outline of said secret.

Now, that doesn't mean much to the official who thinks he or she is in possession of this 'secret,' but it's a veritable treasure to those of us in my profession.

It was pieces such as this that built quite a following for Cratty over the years.

There were few if any columns he used in their first draft, anyway. In fact, he couldn't remember a single instance where the thing had just poured out onto the screen without requiring more than just a little urging and a goodly number of major adjustments.

And, thanks to this latest electronic interruption, this was one more that would be a couple of drafts short of completion.

He was never one to be able to look over a column without some tweaking. If he read over it once finished, he'd always have to add or subtract something. And that was the case every time he called it back up on the screen.

The only time what was on the page was safe was as it rolled off the press.

This day, he had the city's mayor in his sights, a not uncommon topic for his efforts over the previous year and a half here on the southeastern shores of Lake Michigan.

Cratty's talent, if you could really call it that, was a little bit like Mike Royko's, a celebrated journalist who he worked very hard at trying to copy. Royko made his reputation, cutting those in high station down to man on the street size.

And much like Royko, Cratty was a firm believer in that old journalistic admonition to "comfort the afflicted and afflict the comforted."

And he could afflict 'em like few others.

Despite the fact it was probably meant as more of a dig than a compliment, one of his proudest moments came when another journalist once humorously referred to him in print, in a story on the front page of one of Chicago's major papers, as a "Rural Route Royko."

"If Royko doesn't mind, I certainly don't mind," was his comeback to anyone who may have noticed the piece. And, thank God, a lot of people noticed.

That was the time he went head-to-head with a small town's entrenched religious hierarchy. A local woman had opened a female-oriented, new age bookstore across the street from a grade school in Warren, where Cratty was the executive editor – his last stint in Illinois prior to coming to Michigan.

Now, normally there wouldn't have been a fuss. But the grade school's principal was a born-again fundamentalist who saw the devil in just about anything, so much so that she saw the bookstore owner as a member of the occult.

Cratty had more than just a little trouble believing the tale when he'd first heard it. But, sure enough, the principal had marched across the street, stood in the doorway (she refused to come within the walls of this den of iniquity) and accused the business owner of being "heavily into the occult," as she would later describe it.

That wouldn't have been so bad, but she then proceeded to march back to her school and instruct the children – first through sixth graders – through her teachers to steer clear of the bookstore.

Now, Cratty never heard anyone actually explain the reason for this proscription as being "the woman's a witch," but it's certain that the word came up at more than one supper table when the youngsters were explaining everything to their parents that evening.

A column entitled "Education that goes bump in the night" and two editorials later, Cratty was cornered by several department managers at the Warren Reporter News and informed that there were a number of local advertisers who were considering a boycott because of his published ridicule of the situation.

As usual, Cratty refused to back down, and when push came to shove, he offered his resignation but not before explaining that the two sides of the debate consisted of his adversaries claim that the bookstore owner in question was either a witch or this was nothing more than religiously induced hysteria.

Before the smoke had cleared, the flap made it all the way to the airwaves of Chicago – 200 miles away – and the front page of one of the nation's leading newspapers. Cratty was also asked to withdraw his resignation after his employers – a national investors' group – had taken about all the jokes they could stand about the town and its school system being right out of an episode of "Dark Shadows."

Adding to the irony of the situation, oddly, the principal at the center of the "witch story" was also charged with the local school district's upgrade of its computer system. This made it her chore to go to the state capitol and make a pitch for funding for the project.

Cratty simply pointed out in one of his articles that it might be uncomfortable if the principal were asked by state officials if she believed in "witches." And he added that he thought it would be tough for someone whose mindset is trapped somewhere in the 16th century to tackle the 20th-century concept of computers.

Of course, when his hint surfaced that the principal's belief in "witches" might be an obstacle to possible state funding for the community's school district, that virtually threw gasoline on the fire.

"Cratty," came the call from the far end of the Courier newsroom. In all the crash crap, he'd almost forgotten why he was at work an hour or two early.

"Publisher wants you in his office!" shouted Howard Bird, his managing editor and probably the best friend he had on the paper. As he passed Cratty's desk, he pointed to the far end of the building.

"Pat…" began the publisher, *everybody applying the grease to your ass is always just as polite as hell,* Cratty thought to himself, "we're going to have to make some arrangements about your column."

"Such as?" he shot back, never one to spend too much time on preliminaries himself and already catching third gear toward a knock-down, drag-out, shit-kicking contest.

Give and take in the world of business was never one of Cratty's strong suits. He was never one for subtle negotiations, preferring instead to just cut to the chase. It saved a lot of time, and he could use it as just one more occasion when his hard-ass reputation could pick up some added street cred.

"As you probably know by now, we had a visit this morning by a delegation from the mayor's office. He came in, along with the police chief and a couple of assistants…" Cratty wasn't really paying that close attention to the publisher's calendar by this juncture.

No, he did not know about the earlier visit, but wouldn't put it past the small minds at City Hall to try and back door him.

"Well, it shakes down something like this," continued the stuffed shirt of a publisher, who thought he was being cool and droning on as if Cratty really gave a rat's ass.

"They seem to think, and I'm inclined to agree, that your columns – not just the one today but for quite some time as I can tell – are a little, oh, they're sort of out on the edge," said the boss man, who had been in his current post just over four months and seemed to have a talent for understatement as well as kiss-ass diplomacy.

"Are you looking for an argument, or should we both begin by stipulating the obvious here?" retorted Cratty, already at the boiling point. "Yes, my columns are 'out on the edge,' as you put it. And that's precisely why people take the time to read them.

"I was under the impression that that's exactly why we write things to go into this newspaper," he continued. "To have people read them, not just to fill up the ever-greater space between ads. I might point out that by my rough count that space seems to be getting bigger by the day."

He was already in mid-attack just 30 seconds into the conversation.

"Perhaps you'd like to go outside and cool off just a bit before we continue," interjected the publisher. "And while you're out there, call in Howard."

"I'll call him in, but a break isn't going to cool me down. There ain't enough water in that lake," Cratty said, gesturing in the general direction of Lake Michigan just two blocks away, "to cool me off."

"All right, what's going on?" asked Bird as he cleared the door, looking squarely at Cratty and obviously clinging to the hope that he could play mediator, as if there was still something to mediate.

"Well I've just been told that we have to make some 'arrangements'…is that how you put it?" said Cratty, staring at the publisher, "...about my column, whatever that's supposed to mean. I guess you've been called in to explain this in terms even I can understand."

"Now, wait a minute, Pat, this isn't what you've obviously got yourself worked up to believe it is," countered Bird.

"That probably means you two have already reached some sort of an agreement, sans my input," said Cratty in a tone that denoted disgust tinged with more than a shade of indignation. "Look, I don't know what you two have cooked up here..." he continued with very little in the way of a breath.

The newly minted publisher was obviously struck with a sudden idea that Cratty's columns had to either be discontinued or muzzled.

"We thought," continued Bird, "that it might be best if we just sort of cool it for a while on some of your more 'out there' pieces."

"Well, just what did you have in mind?" he asked, now certain that the publisher had gotten his "on the edge" concept from Bird and not really all that concerned with whose ass he'd pulled it out of.

It was one of those lame performances, where the bushwhackers have already practiced their lines only too well and couldn't give 'em with even a hint of sincerity. And Cratty had been bushwhacked by some real pros in his time, so, this duo was certainly out of its depth.

Evidently, the mayor had taken offence to his last column, which meant he'd go absolutely ballistic when and now if the next one hit print.

This one would recount the fact that the mayor had filed a complaint with the county's ambulance service because he thought the sirens were interfering with his sleep and others' late at night in his upscale neighborhood.

Cratty had already started a column on that point, fiddling with a headline something to the effect of "Bring out your dead!"

The result was, there would be a new policy whereby all of Cratty's columns would be submitted first to Bird and then the publisher. The managing editor would edit the items as before and then the publisher would be the final arbiter of just which pieces would go into the newspaper. Of course, to prevent gaping holes on Page 3, Cratty would submit a couple of columns at a time and allow for a selection, as it were.

"Look, just what is it exactly that you don't like about my columns anyway?" he asked, hating himself for being unable to avoid jumping into this petty squabble and knowing he couldn't care less what this guy thought.

This idiot wouldn't know Royko from Ronco.

"I just believe that we shouldn't use the pages of this newspaper to further a personal vendetta," countered the publisher.

"And just what personal vendetta is being furthered in this paper?" continued Cratty, sinking deeper and deeper into the quicksand of an argument he not only couldn't win but had no real intention of winning.

"Well, I just think that your style, almost personally attacking as it were, shows what some might consider just such a vendetta," answered the publisher coolly.

"Now, let me get this straight," Cratty came back, stepping over the boundary between discussion and full-blown assault. "This city's administration comes crying to you because of one of my columns, one of the more innocuous of my career, if I may be allowed to say so, and we cave in because I have a personal vendetta against them?

"The same people who sent a city employee, 500 miles round trip to look into my past in another state, and I've got a personal vendetta?"

"Who did that!" shot back the publisher, who was also closing in on an out-and-out shouting match.

"The mayor whose critique of my work you think so highly of."

"I want to assure you that I come to this discussion without any preconceived notions," insisted the publisher.

"Now hold on, Pat, hear the man out," added Bird, trying desperately to keep himself between the two antagonists – one a new boss he cared for about as much as Cratty did and the other the most popular columnist in his paper and his best friend on the staff.

"I have a couple of packets of information here in my desk that came shortly after I arrived here," explained the publisher. "They're some of the columns you've written here, and I believe back in Illinois? Now, if I'd have wanted to cave in, I would have done it four months ago.

"I don't take anybody else's word for anything," the publisher continued. "I prefer to see things for myself."

"Then I've only got a couple of questions about these so-called 'packets,'" Cratty shot back. "I don't need to ask who sent them, because I already know, despite the fact they most likely came anonymously.

"First, why, if you're not coming to this decision with any preconceived notions, did you keep these so-called 'packets,' and just why are you bringing them up at this particular juncture? And, as for you not taking anybody else's word for anything, just why in hell did you call me in here today if you're so unassailable?"

But their little well-rehearsed one-act play was all for naught and had finally played itself out.

He made it easy for them. He cut his own column – journalistic suicide, so to speak.

"Look, you and I have no real argument here," Cratty announced, suddenly calming down without warning and looking the publisher square in the face. "You don't particularly like my columns, or even the way I write for that matter. So, I see the only agreeable solution here being that I don't write a column for you or this newspaper anymore.

"That's the best way for us to avoid any future unpleasantness. And believe me, if we remain on this course, there will be some unpleasantness ahead."

"Well maybe we should just put this whole thing on ice, so to speak," was the boss's contribution, suddenly realizing that he'd stepped over that thin line between constructive criticism and censorship.

"We can always revisit this decision at a later date," he added with just the right business school smile still hoping to talk Cratty into some sort of compromise.

"The decision has been made," the columnist announced. "If I can't write about any and every individual I happen across in the course of my rounds, I will write about none.

"Just how in the hell could I, in good conscience, go out and write about some miserable, unconnected slob, with him, every other son of a bitch in this town and especially me knowing that the mayor gets a free pass, as well as anybody else's ASS you happen to feel like kissing?" he said as he wheeled on his right foot and burst out the door.

"Why in the fuck does it always come to this point?" he said to himself later for about the umpteenth time. "I always find myself at this same fuckin' crossroad."

Perhaps that was finally the day he should have read the six-foot high writing on the wall. The profession he loved so much and sweated so long over was on the road to ruin.

He was now or was about to be the last of a dying breed in the business. Newspapers weren't run by newspaper people any longer, they were run by a bunch of kiss-ass bean counters who spent all their time pouring over spreadsheets and advertising rates. They didn't give a good goddamn about the people reading their scraps of paper, only pleasing those who paid the advertising bills or were connected.

But like a lotta other suckers in the business, Cratty still had a long hard slog ahead before facing reality.

He'd first come across that sinking feeling of irrelevance in Warren. He'd come to the town that was just 16 miles from his hometown – as close as he ever got to home or at least the only place you could call his "home" during his entire career – as a favor to the guy who was the regional manager of the chain that owned and operated the Livingstone Reader, where he served first as sports editor and then managing editor early in the 1990s.

One of the newspaper chain's VPs had asked if he'd consider coming to his paper at Warren to upgrade its content.

Seems that Cratty's stint at Livingstone had caused quite a stir and bumped up readership and community interest.

Cratty's first question was, "What are you gonna do the first time I tear into somebody you know, are related to or do business with?"

The VP assured him that he could take the heat if it came to that. Cratty didn't say it then, but he knew damned well it would indeed come to that.

It took a couple of years, but it would end like too many of his stops in this business had ended.

3. The Road Guard

He couldn't quite recall just when he'd first seen the guy, sitting along the road outside of a small town in eastern Illinois, or even if he'd first heard the story and then come across the scene. He couldn't even remember when it was that he was first conscious of the sort of legend that had grown up around the man beside the road in Melvin.

It was just a bump in the road, really. Less than a bump. More like a dirt clod. In fact, you could drive that stretch of highway in late June or July and not even see the place for all the wax-like green corn stalks in the way.

Almost as regular as clockwork, come rain, shine this guy would be sitting or walking along the state highway that runs about a quarter-mile or so south of Melvin, between Ello and Eureka. It was someplace Cratty didn't even know existed until he came back from Texas in the early '90s.

He'd only recently returned from an eight-year stint with a newspaper chain in the North Texas area. And, following almost six months out of work, he'd been named editor of a weekly publication in Ellco. He'd never even heard of Ellco, Ill., before being named the editor there, let alone Melvin, six or seven miles further west.

Well, to say that he was merely the editor was to diminish his true status by quite a chunk. He was not only editor of The Ellco Recorder, but also its sports editor, photographer, its total staff and, on occasion, was the one who had to make the weekly drops at the five or six spots in town that sold the publication.

In fact, his role as chief cook and bottle washer at The Recorder was the cause of his getting into opinion writing on a regular basis in the first place.

It was while working at that newspaper that he first dabbled in the art. Oh, he'd written the occasional sports column earlier in his career. But this was the first time he'd actually had to venture opinions on matters from the machinations of the local town council to world events and everything in between.

It took a while to get into the habit of turning out one column each week. But it was a habit he soon liked a lot.

It probably wasn't until that point in his career that he thought he had anything to say, never mind any stories worth telling.

But he found that once he got started, the stories never stopped. He recalled uncomfortable teenage moments with almost crystal clarity, embarrassing school days' fixes and predicaments, and even knock-down-drag-out battles with his father. And those he didn't recall; he discovered a talent for inventing.

It became a weekly religious bloodletting, almost. And it was something akin to an addiction.

Perhaps his greatest knack for the column writing art was his absolute willingness to make fun of himself and just about anyone or anything else.

When all else failed, he'd simply make up a little anecdote to poke fun at himself, and another 20 to 30 inches of white space miraculously disappeared.

However, subtlety was not one of his strengths. As it was said on more than one occasion after that stint in Ellco, "Cratty was never one to let a surgical strike suffice when he had a perfectly serviceable carpet-bombing available." It was almost always a matter of overkill when he sat down at the computer with the purpose of all-out attack in mind.

It was very much like he was two different people – one that wrote about the latest sewing circle or a shop/craft business opening its doors down on Main Street, and another who could wail into the powers that be and all their foibles.

His biggest fear initially was the always-dreaded "writer's block." Of course, he later discovered that such a thing was pure bullshit. But it sure as hell spooked the crap out of him in the beginning.

"What happens if you sit down in front of the typewriter or whatever and just can't come up with anything, no matter how hard you try?"

That was the nightmarish question he constantly asked himself early on.

A guy he looked up to in the business earlier in his career and who was perhaps the best writer he ever knew had some very sound advice on the subject, which, as it turned out, he neither understood completely nor put into practice until he finally had to face a weekly column himself.

"It's a job, not unlike any other. When your old man went off to the factory each day, did you ever hear him ask,

'What if I can't turn out a washing machine or refrigerator today?' You sit down at the typewriter and write. This is just a factory where you get to sit in a chair."

It was a great analogy, and even better, it came from a real newspaper legend. He was the sports editor and former TV sportscaster in a media outfit in an Illinois town along the Mississippi River, and he came from Cratty's hometown where he was a long-time friend of the family. Cratty had worked for the man at his third career stop.

The business was still awash in the noise of typewriter keys and a million other things back then. Between the typewriters banging, wire machines roaring in the background and all the yelling going on, a newsroom sometimes could be as noisy as any factory shop floor.

Likening the newspapers to the refrigerator factory, where Cratty's old man really did put in more than 30 years before retiring, was just the right touch. After that bit of wisdom, he saw the many similarities between the things he and his father did for a living.

But those comparisons never lasted very long. And they disappeared almost entirely after the innovation of the computer in journalism.

In fact, once the racket both figuratively and actually turned to computers, and the hollow, almost imperceptible noise of the keyboard turned the decibel level down to a mere fraction of its former self, it was hard to still think of the job in terms of a factory and, for a while at least, get used to the near silence.

"Hey, can you people keep it down to a dull roar over there?" he'd heard a rookie, who was trying to turn out a story on deadline. "Some of us are trying to work."

"Well, FNG (Fuckin' New Guy), if you wanted to write in a vacuum, you should go to the public library. And while you're at it, you can kiss my loud ass," Cratty blurted out. "I've got more time in this chair than you've got on this Earth."

But, no matter how noisy things either got or didn't get, Cratty never seemed to run out of fodder.

He also never seemed to deplete the amount of controversy that usually accompanied that fodder and his spreading of it.

"I just can't believe that you'd let someone say the things this Cratty fella' puts down on paper," said one of his detractors, not long after he got in the swing of column writing.

"Why, he's always writing something or other of a negative nature."

"What will people think of us when they read this stuff?" asked another.

Cratty would always harken back to the words of his favorite 20th-century author, George Orwell, when bombarded by such criticism: "Journalism is printing what someone else does not want printed; everything else is public relations."

At first, he used to wind himself up to a near nervous breakdown with some of his pieces.

"Have I got this nailed down? What if I missed this, or that?" He'd worry himself into about two days without sleep in those early ventures. Until it was in print and on the street, Cratty couldn't close his eyes.

It really used to bother him. He'd finish up a particularly explosive piece after 10 to 15 phone calls, four or five drafts, and then be unable to sleep while his insides literally churned and bubbled from all the anxiety.

And usually, his top concern was something to the effect that he hadn't expended every bit of ammunition on the target.

There was another thing about the way Cratty wrote columns; once the piece was put to bed, that was it. He wasn't going back to toss in some added digs, tie up loose ends or whatever. If it was on the page, he barely ever read it. It was ancient history.

But you could be damn sure the objects of his efforts would read them over and over again. In fact, in their tirades on the phone – very few people have the guts to face you with their counter-attacks – he found that they remembered every word better than the author.

His first major expose came during a sheriff's race back in about 1993. The weekly chain he was working for, where he had already risen to general manager, was purchased by the chain that owned both the Livingstone Reader and Warren Reporter News.

Seems there was a young detective on the local sheriff's department who was bucking for the county's top law enforcement job. But the guy had a couple of gigantic flaws – he was rabidly vindictive and a notorious drunken womanizer. He was so vindictive that he once threatened another deputy on the force in a written note. He made no bones about it.

To make things worse, he proceeded to trump up some criminal charges against this other deputy and a business associate, going so far as to raid the pair's auto salvage operation and confiscate their books.

All this didn't really amount to much until the popular county sheriff suddenly died a few months before a primary election. The vindictive sheriff's deputy, who hadn't exactly wasted his time in the ranks, suddenly emerged as the leading successor with the help of several pieces of somewhat embarrassing information on some very important county movers and shakers he'd accumulated over the years.

The local Republican Party machine, the only political organization with any chance in hell of electing anyone was, almost overnight, all hot to promote this elective newcomer for sheriff.

Cratty got a call late one night while he was sitting around the Livingstone newspaper office, where he'd just been named executive editor and his career as a poisoned-pen columnist kicked into high gear.

Three or four months later, the sheriff's deputy was soundly trounced by a political outsider in the primary. Of course, this followed a string of front-page blockbusters that completely unmasked the climbing deputy and his department supporters and painted them as little more than cheap thugs.

The GOP hierarchy was in a complete meltdown after that defeat. It led to a judge – a leading Republican in the county – regaling juries with rants about the Reader's editor and his style.

It almost bordered on an obsession and was seen in some local circles as downright unhinged.

In one of his first editorial offerings at Livingstone shortly after taking over in early 1994 and during the hottest stages of the sheriff's race debate, Cratty enlisted his readers in the job of taking part in their community:

We've done our job, now you do yours

Now that we have your attention, we'd like to hear from you, the citizens.

We know that there are many of our readers who disagree with the recent tone we've sounded in this space and on our front page. There are still more who are offended by the issues raised. And another sizeable group is probably pleased with what they read.

Believe it or not, all of these reactions either extreme or everything in between are exactly what we had in mind when we sat in front of the computer screen.

The job of a newspaper, contrary to what many might think, is to raise topics for discussion and public scrutiny. And we have a near sacred obligation to expose the character, acts, and intentions of public officials.

It's not true that Cratty's column approach was picked up that first winter back from Texas. He'd actually started as an investigative reporter – a very new field back then – in the early 1970s.

He'd picked up most of what he was now practicing in eastern Illinois back then.

It was Cratty and another reporter, who wasn't all that far removed from his beginnings in the business as well at the time, formed an investigative reporting team in the first few years of the '70s.

Cratty never spared the whip, that's for sure. The pair of them would gather all their copious notes and memories, trudge over to a far corner of the newsroom and do what they did best – type, cajole, plead, and scream for what would seem hours on end, until they could turn in a good 20 to 30 inches of what always seemed – to them, at least – as "cream copy."

It took a while for Cratty to do quite the same volume of work individually.

And it was always very hard to describe just how they did it.

One would sit down at the typewriter, the other standing over his shoulder, and the process would begin.

The lead was always the hardest part of the process. Neither of the two was capable of simply explaining his differences of opinion with the product on the page, he would just nudge the current typist out of the way and start a new lead or passage a few returns later.

That's the way it used to go. Sometimes, the guy seated would actually get a couple or three paragraphs on the page before being rudely interrupted.

It took Cratty a few false starts when he finally had to write by himself. But he found that he was quite capable of doing it himself, even though he always missed the camaraderie and banter.

Local legend back in Woodbury County had it that the guy along the highway outside of Melvin was a shell-shocked Viet Nam vet, who lived with his mother and was a basket case on VA disability.

There was no other family that anyone had heard of, or maybe they'd up and left the guy because of his unusual lifestyle. At least that was one theory. And all he did was traipse up and down the roadway, unperturbed by the cars whizzing past in either direction.

"Yeah, he's supposed to be some 'Nam vet who lives on a disability and sits watching life zoom by on the highway," the police chief in Ellco once told Cratty. "I've seen him I don't know how many times. The fucker's crazy."

From the first time Cratty had seen him – a guy he could easily tell was just about his own age – there seemed a very strange kinship. He felt attached in some way.

It was almost as if he could have sat down, talked with the guy like they were long lost friends, and each would have understood all there was to know about the other, like they'd picked up the exact conversation they'd started 20 years before.

When it came to other guys who'd been over the pond, that's the way it seemed to be for Cratty.

He could sit down and trade stories and thoughts with any other 'Nam vet, regardless of branch of service, and it was like they'd known each other all their natural lives. It was an instant connection.

It made no difference whatsoever, the color of the man's skin, twang in his speech or social standing, Cratty could immediately communicate with another Viet Nam vet.

Call it shared experience, mutual respect or mental disability, but he could strike up a conversation with anybody who'd ever been "in-country" ('Nam), and hit it off from the first sound out of their mouths.

And that was part of the connection with the guy along the side of the road. Cratty didn't know what he really felt about this guy he'd only seen and never really met. But it was a sure thing that he didn't quite see it the same as the thousands of others who must have viewed and been a little startled or more likely felt sorry for the same ghost-like figure beside the highway.

This weird sixth sense or instant recognition could hit at the strangest times.

He was once driving in the dead of winter in downtown Chicago, where a guy was standing in the snow and sub-zero weather holding up a handwritten sign: "VIET NAM VET, WILL WORK FOR FOOD."

The scene caused him to pull his car over in a driving snowstorm, climb out and hand the guy every cent he had on him, 25 or 30 bucks, then insist the guy climb into his car and accept a ride to a shelter. That mental picture also haunted him for months after the incident.

Was it pity or was it fear? Did he see this seemingly lost soul standing in the weeds or sitting in a lawn chair by the road as a victim perhaps of many of the same tempests that blew inside of him? Was he someone he should feel sorry for or someone who should make him feel sorry for himself?

Was the guy completely lost in a schizophrenic haze of flashing lights and misfiring nerve endings? Or did he see him as somebody who knew something Cratty or the rest of the world didn't?

Did this guy, staring almost blankly at the passing cars, look out on all he surveyed with amazement or contempt? Was it a case of no connection to reality, or – something Cratty feared even more – was he all too aware of just where

Cratty and the rest of the world rushing past was really headed?

As all the so-called regular world marched past, was this guy beside the road the one who already knew the meaning of life? Did he have all the answers the others in their air-conditioned, bank-owned, and brightly colored vehicles were quickly scurrying to find?

Cratty was always going to stop his car one of these days and engage the guy along the road in a conversation. There was something either he or the guy could impart.

Because deep down inside, Cratty himself was starting to see things, especially those things surrounding his stint in 'Nam, a lot differently. The further he got away from the most defining 12 months of his almost 50 years of life, the closer he got to what he really felt about that war.

In the 15 years and two marriages between about 1975 and his coming to Ellco, Cratty had done an almost complete flip-flop on the war. He'd gone from a total "hawk," a real reactionary, to almost the other side of the spectrum.

He was angry. And that anger would start expressing itself in some very interesting ways. And one of the chief ways would be in the things he would write.

After the late 1970s, Cratty would find it very hard to feel anything remotely resembling respect for the so-called duly constituted authority of his community, state, or nation. And, as for patriotism, that was something that would conjure very little in the heart of this Midwestern boy who'd quit high school a year before graduation and joined up to go "kill a commie for Christ" back in the spring of 1964.

He respected very little and, at the absolute bottom of that shortlist – no, failing to even make any list at all – was his country.

Perhaps that's why he was such a caustic writer. He just couldn't seem to bring himself to not print for all the world to see when those in authority were either abusing their position or just was too damned incompetent to perform their duty.

"Cratty, so why ya' on my case so damn much?" one of his adversaries had once asked. "It's like I done sumpthin' to ya' personal or sumpthin'."

He tried to explain to the guy – who was playing the role of a hood wannabe from the Chicago suburbs who was overseeing a small horse racing operation – that it was nothing personal, just business. Cratty had originally taken up the post of racing writer on the publication's sports staff, where he eventually hooked up with the paper's regular investigative reporter on a series of pieces regarding the local facility.

"Look, Cratty, I'm a human being jus' like you," said the track general manager. "I gotta' family, jus' like you. Maybe you should tink' a dat' sometime?"

He often remembered that telephone conversation in later years, especially when some new city, county, or state official or business type was spotlighted for some sort of stupidity in one of his columns and then tried to conjure up some kind of edge with thinly veiled or open threats.

"Look, I've been threatened by professionals, friend," Cratty would calmly reply. "In fact, I've had hints of threats that gave me more of a reason to be concerned."

He'd stand at his desk – bright red Texas Rangers hat cocked coolly forward on his head for the rest of his career after his eight years in Dallas-Fort Worth – and just spout off. He could care less who was listening and seemed more like a stand-up comedian or disgruntled old man who'd just been turned out of a bar following an altercation.

"I'm not talking to any more assholes today," he would say. "So, anybody fielding any calls for me, just simply make it clear upfront that I have no time on my agenda for shit-stains."

Nobody else in the room understood or cared to understand. But then he seemed to make a lot of comments that were taken in much the same manner by colleagues.

It'd been like that for years now. Everybody just seemed to steer clear of Cratty, and especially when he was taking a random walk on the edge of what they believed was his already delicate sanity. At least that's what everybody thought.

Most of the people who knew Cratty professionally, which is the same as saying not at all, gave him plenty of leeway.

Perhaps they were afraid that the longhaired old white man in the red hat, which he wore everywhere and on every given occasion – save the church and the funeral home – might have some sort of Viet Nam flashback.

Of course, he wouldn't, but he sort of liked to cultivate the myth that he just might.

He spent a lot of his time actually trying to encourage his co-workers to believe that he was just crazy enough to be really dangerous. A lot of his efforts in recent years were turned toward projecting the angry old man image. He worked very hard at building just such a persona.

Fortunately, or unfortunately, depending on your circumstance or connection to the self-proclaimed son of a bitch, he wasn't anywhere near as dangerous as he liked to make people believe.

His oldest daughter had ratted him out once in Texas.

He was holding an entire back shop hostage with a harangue one night when his oldest came in behind him. While the entire staff cowered in the corner, she immediately destroyed the effect with, "I don't know how anyone can take that man seriously."

His daughters might be the only two individuals on earth who really knew Cratty. And he was not the least bit sorry about that.

After all, their mother was one of just two people in this world who could push every button on him instantaneously. So, it all sort of evened out.

At the root of his ever-increasing anger in recent years was the fact that his old man had been right. And he'd been too goddamned proud and stubborn to admit it before Pat E. Cratty passed away while his oldest son was still in Texas.

He'd had a terrible go-round with Pop when he came to the old man to ask him to sign the enlistment consent during his junior year in high school.

He'd eventually badgered him into signing, but not before receiving an ominous warning: "The day'll come when these tin-horn politicians and fake heroes will turn everything you hold dear into shit."

Then his old man added, "I don't wanna hear a word about this, ever again. Not one word of complaint. You go off, serve your stint, and keep your mouth shut. Whatever happens, it'll serve ya' right."

Of course, his Pop didn't really mean it. He was as pissed as he'd ever been at his eldest son. And he hadn't ever envisioned giving up that son to the United States Army.

His father had fought in World War II. He knew exactly what lay ahead for his son, but he had never thought for a single moment that the younger Cratty would really end up in the Army, let alone a combat zone.

But all that was still somewhere down the line – the fervor, the disappointment, the exultation, the shame, the pride, and finally the anger, which was probably the first sign of PTSD.

There would be one hell of a lot of anger.

He'd get madder and madder without really knowing just why.

No, he'd never quite managed to stop and talk to the guy beside the road near Melvin. One commitment led to another, and every time he found himself in the neighborhood, he just never remembered.

But there was any number of times he'd wished he had.

Just before he'd been so rudely interrupted by his "concerned" publisher the day before, Cratty was in the process of putting the finishing touches on a column about the mayor of Indiana City and his $50,000 home remodeling job, which was believed to have been given gratis by a construction firm that had and continued to do business with the city.

As he rolled into work the next morning, he knew there'd be no telephone calls arising from that column. It would never appear, owing to his sudden pronouncement of the day before.

He'd learned something if he'd learned nothing else in his column exploits over the years.

Every town is basically the same, it's just the names of the miscreants, misfits, manipulators, movers, and morons that changed, along with the city limit signs. Each and every community on this planet has a class of people who, when elected and/or appointed to any position of responsibility, immediately finds it necessary to become a double-dealing, deceitful asshole.

As the old saying goes, "Power corrupts and absolute power corrupts absolutely." But Cratty had come up with an addendum: "Power also makes pretentious pricks out of otherwise passable personages."

4. A Naked Lady

"Pat Cratty is one of those rare individuals who is principled to a fault. Given a choice between what everybody else in the entire world may see as a minor point of principle, Cratty will invariably end up choosing the principle and standing behind it even to his own detriment."

Those words "principled to a fault" – one of the entries submitted to the State University placement office and written by one of his professors his last quarter in school – would end up being both the bane and the reward of his entire career.

They would lead him to the highest professional praise and the lowest possible depths. They would strain three marriages far past the breaking point and make him a journeyman apprentice in the newspaper business, traveling from publication to publication and rarely if ever staying anywhere long enough to be vested in a retirement plan.

And now those words had sent him on still another job search. One good thing about it, it kept his resume writing skills sharp. He could turn out a seven-page resume at the drop of a hat, usually the red one with the big white "T" on top of his head.

"Sometimes it takes six months, a year or even two. Sooner or later, I get crossways with my superiors over something I'm always convinced is a point of principle," he was telling himself once again.

"Of course, they never see it that way. But I can never seem to see it any other way," he said to himself, as always for about the ten-zillionth time in his career.

It had ended at Warren in much the same manner.

Hell, the outgoing mayor, city clerk, and at least one council member had even gone behind closed doors and ended up filing suit against Cratty in Warren. They were just certain that his "in your face" style of journalism would unhinge the entire power structure. And, as it so happened, it wound up doing just that.

A political newcomer squared off with the town's sitting mayor and upended the so-called experts by winning. In fact, before the smoke had cleared, the mayor, city clerk and one of four incumbent members of the City Council were all out on their asses, following months of Cratty attacks on the city's power structure.

That must have been the "dirt" the Michigan mayor's stooges brought back from Warren.

Of course, Cratty had caught the hacks at it when they started looking into his past. He'd caught 'em at it and then spent another of his columns turning them on the spit.

The disgruntled city fathers' lawsuit from Warren would languish for a few years and eventually be settled for a fraction of the asking price by the insurance company, which could have probably waited the whole thing out but for the lawyers' fees.

Three to four years earlier, the publisher at Warren's Reporter News was also one of the VPs for the investment group that owned the paper in Livingstone, and he asked

Cratty if he wouldn't consider coming to his publication which he felt needed a content boost.

He was looking for a boost in readership and was more than a little impressed with the way Cratty had livened things up in Livingstone.

At the end of their first conversation, in 1994 Cratty warned the publisher about the residual effects that usually came along with his arrival in any new community.

But the guy, like all the rest, totally underestimated the consternation and was more than willing to accept the risk. But, as Cratty had found out far too many times, that's what they all say 'til the shit hits the fan. Of course, adding to the attraction of the new position was the fact that Cratty was about to embark on his third marriage – a huge mistake as it would turn out – to a school teacher in his hometown, which was just east of Warren.

Looking back on it, Cratty should have chucked both the wedding and the job offer. But, once again, he mistakenly thought he'd met just the right woman and professional situation.

That was back when he still believed the newspaper business could be rescued from itself and might still be everything he'd once thought it should be. He just needed to find the right broadsheet to perfect his dream.

Instead, he was starting to see it for what it really was: a daily and/or weekly dose of laudanum wrapped in paper and just literary enough not to confuse the advertisers' potential customers with what was really going on.

By this time, he should have wised up. But that was still years down the road.

He should have been worried that this was the 10th such search in 25 years. But he just couldn't ever seem to get his mind around the fact that he was riding a lame horse in a race that had long since ended. He wouldn't figure that out for another 18 or so years and a couple more stops.

The newspaper business had lost its way, trading readers for advertisers. Now, bean counters ran publications, and newsrooms were simply filled with the underpaid college grads who covered up the white space between the moneymaking object of the exercise. The revenue tail wagged the dog, which surrendered its credibility to those who paid the bills.

"Hello, Jacob," said the matronly voice on the other end of the phone. "Don't you call your mother anymore?" she asked.

He'd spent the first 17 and a half years of his life being called "Jacob," his middle name. If someone had ever called his home while his dad was still alive and asked for "Pat Cratty," they'd have been put on the line with his old man, the only "Pat Cratty" in the house as far as anyone else knew at the time.

Cratty had been named for his father and a football player of some renown, who would also serve as his godfather.

It would have been awkward calling two people in the same household by the same name, so he naturally picked up Jacob and more usually, Jake.

He couldn't remember just when he realized that his first name was not Jacob, and in fact, his first Social Security card was issued to Jacob Patrick Cratty – a predicament he'd be forced to correct at a local post office just a couple of years before his eventual retirement.

Who knows, maybe that's why he seemed to give everybody a nickname.

He could separate everybody he knew in his life by what they called him – "Pat or P.J.," for all those who knew him after age 17, or "Jake," up to that age. And with his bad memory for regular names and faces, that slight edge came in handy more than once.

"How's it going, Mom?" he asked, only casually engaged in the conversation.

"Fine! I just called to see if you'd bothered to sign the divorce papers that Beth sent you?"

Oh shit, he'd forgotten to open that large manila envelope that came by special delivery. That's what was probably inside. In all the chaos swirling in Michigan of late, he'd completely forgotten about the divorce.

"As a matter of fact, I hadn't quite gotten around to it, Mother!" he said, now making it up as he went along.

His third wife deserved a lot better. Elizabeth was a great woman who got tangled up in a relationship with a self-absorbed newspaper hack. Cratty couldn't think past his next assignment and always sank himself much too deeply into anything that came across his desk and caught his fancy. It didn't matter if it was a half-baked telephone tip from somebody who had nothing better to do with their life than to eat cheese on someone they had a paranoid obsession with. Or it could be a letter from a seemly insignificant character whose only possession in this world was that one piece of dirt on a local paragon of political and/or social virtue.

And there were always plenty of those kinds of people to go around. In fact, it was his considered opinion that every crossroads in this world had a mob of just such individuals. It was just a matter of turning over enough rocks until you found one.

His journalism style attracted the seamier side of life wherever he landed. He soon found that his job was much like that of a water faucet – once you twisted the handle, the tips just kept pouring.

Readers were just waiting for someone who could level the playing field, or so they thought. Somebody who could keep the lights on so as to deny the cockroaches a place to hide.

He'd started the divorce in 1995 just before leaving for the job in Michigan, and after a failed reconciliation and false restart would finally wind up the process, as luck would have it, just as he was exiting the shores of Lake Michigan.

The last two of Cratty's divorces, unlike his first, came at his insistence. It really does get easier after that first 1,250-footstep from the back of a plane.

Suddenly, his mind rolled back to that intersection just outside of Melvin. There was a click and he was back in 'Nam. His unit was convoying between Cam Ranh Bay and Na Trang along Highway 1 up to the Vietnamese coast.

"Road guards out," came the command and the troopers on the two ends of the first line of every unit, would run out to the next intersection and stand at parade rest to halt the cross traffic.

He distinctly remembered a naked, elderly woman standing on a cement kilometer marker shouting what sounded like epithets at the passing G.I.s, none of whom could understand a word she was saying. Strange thing is, nobody ever mentioned the incident that day or later.

It was like everybody was having the same bad dream and either didn't need to repeat it for fear he was undergoing a complete mental breakdown or was hallucinating in the steamy Southeast Asian heat.

He finally knew why the guy along the highway in Illinois had such a compelling hold on him.

"Hey, D.C., can you find people on the internet?" he asked of a colleague, displaying his absolute ignorance as far as computers were concerned.

D.C.'s real name was Nicolett, but like just about everybody else he'd come to know and like in his life, he simply preferred to use a nickname. And if they had none, he would just create one.

Actually, D.C. created her own moniker. The initials were derived from her ubiquitous derogatory comment on others: "Dork Chop."

Cratty had a nickname for just about everybody he had any semblance of a relationship with on this earth.

And those who didn't have a nickname he just referred to as "Bud."

It got to the point that any even half-assed imitation or spoof of Cratty had to contain the phrase "I'll be go-ta' hell," or an endless succession of sentences that ended with "Bud."

"Yes, Cratty," D.C. came right back with some of her Muskegon, Mich. sarcasm.

"And, in case you haven't heard, President Kennedy was assassinated in Dallas, Texas, of all places," she added just for emphasis.

That's probably what he liked most about D.C.: she was him 25 years ago in a skirt.

"Cut the crap D.C., nobody likes a smart ass. Besides, you weren't even a yen in your ole' man's pants when Kennedy was assassinated.

"Just show me how this thing works, so as I can find somebody," he said, sitting down at the one terminal in the newsroom that he knew was always hooked up to the internet.

Even at his age in the mid-90s, he was determined to learn this computer shit after all.

"OK, OK, just tell me how to get this goddamned thing going?" he said in his usual growl. "I need to get to someplace where they can find someone for me."

"Keep your shirt on, Cratty," cautioned D.C. "Have a little patience." He clicked the cursor onto the Netscape home page's "internet search."

"All right, all right. Now, what do I do?"

"Type in the first and last name of the person you're looking for."

D E B O N I S, he typed, his fingers uncharacteristically fumbling over the keys.

He'd known the guy as Verne, but somehow it slipped his mind at that moment. And, as it would turn out, that would delay the search for several years.

"What if I'm not sure about the first name, D.C."

"Leave it out. But don't forget to put in a city and a state."

KANSAS CITY, MISSOURI, he added in the box indicated for that purpose.

"Now, click on to 'Search,'" she added.

"Shit! How come this damn thing takes so goddamn long, anyway? I'll be go-ta' hell, I could walk house to house in the entire state of Missouri faster than this thing's getting' me there.

"Jesus," he said after about five minutes of watching the clock go around on his cursor. "1,004 matches. How in the crap am I supposed to wade through that many choices?"

"Cratty, I don't like this at all, man," DeBonis announced the night before a very odd mission.

The idea was to send a team of 40 to 50 men some 10 to 15 miles into an area southwest of Tuy Hoa. They were to travel along and just on the other side of the Song Ba River, which ran from the highlands inland to the central coast. The objective was a suspected POW camp, where some Americans were believed to be held.

The mission was a helicopter insert, some five to 10 klicks short of the objective, make a hit-and-run strike on the camp, spring any Americans and then beat it to a landing zone where choppers would extract the whole group. Or at least what was left of the group.

That was the plan, but it seemed much too sketchy to have been on the drawing board for any length of time, if it had been there at all. More than likely the whole deal was the half-baked idea of some John Wayne of a staff officer bucking for a desk job in Saigon.

At any rate, the mission was to jump off late in the afternoon the next day.

It was really the only time that Cratty remembered DeBonis' cocky self-assurance wavering.

And he wasn't alone. Cratty himself had a bad feeling about this one as well.

The feeling was so strong that he actually wrote a rather emotional letter back home, as if to soften the blow of the bad luck he was almost certain would befall him.

They always say, of the world famous "They Always Say," that a guy knows when he's gonna get it.

Never before that particular night, and at no time since, had Cratty had that feeling.

He wondered if DeBonis had that same feeling the night before his own death decades later. And then he cussed himself for having the thought. He'd often been that way, almost tempting fate in his mind. Having thoughts, he knew he shouldn't have, but having them just the same.

He never once really thought that he'd die during his tour of duty. Some 25 years later, he remembered that distinctly. In fact, he was just as certain that nothing bad was going to happen to him, except for that one night trying to catch a little sleep before the platoon-size helicopter assault across the Song Ba.

He hated to start the humiliating job search process once again. He'd worked for several different newspapers in his almost 27 years by that point. And he had only once in all that time improved himself by changing jobs.

It seemed like every time he made a switch; it was for less money.

When he left northwest Illinois, in 1982, it was after he'd been laid off. From there he went to Texas, but not

68

until he'd sat on his ass for a couple of months looking for work.

He'd only happened on the Texas job while he was down visiting his brother while recuperating from his first marathon.

He wouldn't even have caught on in Texas if he hadn't known a guy who knew a guy.

One of the guys he'd gone to college with – a kid who first got him into journalism while the two were going to State – told him to look up a fella he'd known in the racket.

"Look, Cratty, you've got nothing to lose," said the college buddy, who was then a member of the administrative staff at the pair's old college. "While you're down in Dallas, give Hal Huston a call.

"He's some big wig with a suburban newspaper chain down in there. If you're going down to see your brother anyway, just give him a call.

"It can't hurt."

Huston had spent a couple of years as publisher at the LaMotte paper, where Cratty had started in the business. Of course, he never knew the guy because Huston's stretch in LaMotte came several years after Cratty had moved on.

Well, "hurt" it did not. In fact, it turned into an eight-year gig, his longest stay anywhere to that point. He also managed to make the best money to that point of his career.

Of course, he had to add a little stringing, but it was a pretty good gig, all things considered.

Looking back on it later, he couldn't for the life of him figure out just why he'd ever come back to Illinois from Texas.

Well, there was the matter of not having a job following another layoff. But still, he could have stayed on, there was enough freelance work from AP and others to keep him eating.

But no, Cratty was the kind of guy who just had to have a clock to punch each and every day. He was not what they call, in the classified jobs section, "a self-starter." He wasn't happy unless he was tied to a payroll. It wasn't as if he couldn't write and turn out copy on his own. He just couldn't function unless he was in a noisy newsroom and there was a deadline hanging over his head.

He desperately needed somebody to give him orders.

That's probably why he had formed such close ties with his platoon sergeant in Viet Nam.

William Davis was a soldier's soldier, an airborne Ranger from southeastern Ohio who never really found a home until he joined the Army.

It probably had something to do with the fact that Cratty was looking for a father figure after having left the one he had back home at age 17.

When he left home, he really didn't think too much of his father. In fact, he was downright embarrassed by him. His dad was a bit of a drinker, and Cratty was under the mistaken impression it reflected on him.

His high school sweetheart's family wasn't very impressed with "Cratty," and he was just certain his dad's exploits from time to time in the local paper had something to do with it.

That's why he and DeBonis had formed such a tight bond in 'Nam. DeBonis was named after a father he didn't care much for and refused to go by Verne, instead assuming the identity of John, his middle name. In fact, DeBonis was the only guy Cratty knew after joining the Army that ever called him "Jake."

"Why in the hell would you want to come back here?" his dad had asked when he'd informed him, he was trying to move back to Illinois from Texas in about 1989.

"Hell, you've got the best job in the world," said Pop. "Aren't any big-league baseball teams to cover back here."

Pop really did think Cratty had the best job in the world? He was covering Major League Baseball for the AP in Texas and also had stints covering the Dallas Cowboys and NBA franchise as well.

Hell, covering sports at all and getting paid for it was what his old man considered a dream job all right, especially since he spent over three decades on the assembly line at a home appliance factory.

Cratty still recalled the day he'd taken his father to a Big Ten football game.

He had only been in the business about two or three years when he was sent to cover the contest.

It's certainly the softest gig in sports.

You sit on your ass for two and a half to three hours, while the sports information staff does everything but hold your dick when you're taking a piss.

They have "play-by-play" and complete stats run off almost while the teams are switching ends. A college kid comes along every few minutes asking if you'd like something to eat or drink.

The only thing remotely like work is the hour or so of hectic action that follows the final horn when everybody in the press box is scrambling around trying to file for the early

Saturday evening deadline by phone in those days before computers.

"Is this all you do for a living?" his father asked, in one of his few complete sentences on game day.

Pop was not a big talker.

"Yeah, Pop, this is all I do for a living," he told the old man, who almost cracked a smile.

It was that afternoon, early in his career, when it finally struck him that his father was proud that his eldest son could say, "This is all I do for a living."

When he later spent those eight years from 1982 to 1990 in Texas, the old man would come down and visit, coming to see both him and his younger brother. When he would come, usually during the summer, Cratty would always swing seats right up front at Texas Rangers games, which he usually had to cover anyway.

Pop loved his baseball. And he really loved his Cubs.

But after the Cubs, the Rangers were just fine in his book, especially when his oldest son could get him in the main level box seats set aside for press guests like he was somebody special.

"We aren't very good," his father had informed him after a particularly bad outing by the Rangers. With that statement, his father had said it all.

He was referring to the editorial "WE," in the sense that he believed his son was a part of the ballclub, and he too, in some small way, was as well.

"No, Pop, we ain't very good," Cratty agreed.

Of course, implied in his father's question several years later about why he was trying to find a job back in Illinois was the elder Cratty's dislike of his son's high school sweetheart, Rebecca. The old man knew the reason for this sudden wish to come back to the bitter Midwest winters and sinus headaches because he knew the two were once again seeing each other.

It was Rebecca. It was always Rebecca.

Pop did not like Rebecca, the girl who he blamed for giving his oldest boy a somewhat poor self-image as a teenager.

Rebecca, whose folks never thought his eldest son was good enough. Her parents made no secret of their displeasure with their daughter's choice in young men.

Come to think of it, if it hadn't been for Rebecca, Cratty would never have been to Viet Nam in the first place.

It was something he had to prove to not only himself but to Rebecca's parents.

He was hell-bent on proving he was good enough for this sandy-haired and somewhat awkward girl from the north side of town.

They'd met as freshmen, and following a bit of a jerky start – he initially was interested in one of her friends – they became the classic romance of the Class of 1965. Of course, Cratty wouldn't really be around for the finish of the Class of '65. But Cratty and Rebecca were certainly one of the classic high school romances in town during the early 1960s.

He often thought that every honor he'd ever sought and won, every plateau reached was another attempt to prove himself good enough for the first love of his life – and her parents.

"Why Jacob, we have nothing against you," Rebecca's stepmother had told Cratty on the phone once when the gutsy kid had simply called to try to plead his own case.

"You're not quite what we had in mind for Rebecca," said the snooty woman, whom he'd probably go to his grave detesting.

It was that obvious blow to his son's ego that had caused Cratty's father to come to dislike the girl. And perhaps it was that very fact that accounted for a lot of the relationship between father and son, at least during his teen years.

As it turned out, he didn't wind up moving back to Illinois from Texas just yet. And he wouldn't do so until the late fall of 1990, a full 15 months after his father had died of a heart attack in the late summer of 1989.

But when Cratty finally did come back to Illinois, it would have been with his late father's approval. He and Rebecca, who had finally managed to rekindle their teenage love affair between marriages in the late 1980s, had once again gone their separate ways.

Rebecca had found someone who was a little more what her parents had in mind – and as it turned out what she really had in mind as well.

Cratty always prided himself as being a pretty good judge of people. And that was probably true, except when it came to a teenage sweetheart, whom he thought was the one female God had intended him for.

No one – not his father, friends, any of his three wives or any other woman on earth, for that matter – could dissuade him of that idea.

But, when they finally found each other again, after some 22 years, it turned out that she wasn't a whole lot different from her parents. The same vision they had in mind for her was indeed the same one she seemed to have for herself.

She wound up engaged – they would marry several years later – to a retired, mid-level Caterpillar executive some 10 years older who was able to give her most of the material comforts she ever wanted.

Those were certainly not things she was ever going to get from Cratty. At the rate he was going, from job to job and town to town, there was some doubt that he could provide any kind of material security for himself let alone another wife.

5. Stirring Shit

The news came about mid-day on the scheduled jump-off: "The mission's a scrub." There would be no piss poor planned daring rescue raid on a Viet Cong prison camp.

No platoon of Screamin' Eagles had been any happier since relief broke through at Bastogne a day after Christmas in 1944.

"You know, you people are really pathetic," said Sgt. Richard C. Moyer, the first smiling face with sergeant's stripes attached that Cratty came across in his military career.

It was basic, Fort Knox, in June 1964.

Moyer was the drill instructor who would shepherd Cratty and 43 other recruits through boot camp. He was a World War II veteran, and had spent most of his 25-plus years in "This Man's Army," as a paratrooper. He'd been just about every conceivable enlisted rank in the Army, and he had the shadows on the sleeves of his fatigues to prove it.

Sgt. Moyer, as he so often liked to admit, was at Bastogne with the 101st, more affectionately known as the "One Oh Worst," that December when tanks from Patton's Third Army broke through to lift the siege that was the product of Hitler's last gasp of World War II: The Battle of The Bulge.

And, as Moyer was so fond of remembering, whenever one of his recruits seemed to reach the breaking point, "Why I once had to stand inspection arms in the sub-zero temperatures of Bastogne with snow up to my ass, my stomach pushing against my backbone and my hands numb from frostbite. So, don't start cryin' ta' me about your goddamn aches and pains, troop!"

And then he'd usually punctuate his speeches with: "Jesus baldheaded Christ, you people are the biggest bunch of momma's boys and fuck-ups I ever had the misfortune of meeting."

He wondered all of a sudden what had ever happened to Moyer, who was a lot more human than he liked to let on. And he'd probably met just as many "momma's boys" and "fuck-ups" each and every eight-week basic training cycle.

"I'm here to teach you sorry-ass recruits how to kill Russians and Chinese," Moyer would announce every chance he got. And he meant it, too.

Moyer's understanding of world affairs and politics was no more complicated than that. Take a group of American teens, dress 'em up in olive drab and steel pots, hand 'em a rifle, some ammunition and point 'em at the enemy.

As a child of his times, Cratty was certainly open to such a worldview, having spent more than his share of time ducking and covering under a flimsy school desk during atomic bomb drills. Hell, when he was a sophomore in high school, he was chomping at the bit to run off and join the fight during that fateful October of the 1962 Cuban Missile

Crisis. Moyer was right. The Cold War world was just that simple.

Cratty wondered more recently how Sgt. Moyer would navigate the streets of America in the 21st century. What would he make of enemies without uniforms and fueled by religious rather than political ideologies?

He'd have certainly found a way to survive such a world, but for his generation, it would have been a very confusing one indeed.

Moyer was Cratty's first point of contact with the United States Army. And he or someone just like him probably welcomed every single recruit in every army on the planet.

"Publisher wants ta' see ya', Cratty," called the city editor.

He was becoming an almost daily visitor in the corner office toward the front of the newsroom, and he didn't really like it one bit.

The less he saw or heard from this publisher, or any publisher for that matter, the easier his life would be.

Maybe it was his natural distrust of "business," as such. Or perhaps it was just his inability to relate to people in suits. But Cratty did not get along with bean counters.

There was a time when publishers at most papers at least had a working knowledge of the creative side. But not anymore.

It was awfully hard, in these days of buyouts, mergers, chain papers, and consolidations, to find a publisher with any newsroom experience. In fact, he hadn't come across one in years.

They weren't a dying breed; they were long since extinct.

"Them goddamn 'igits in Chicago," boomed Mr. Randolph's deep voice across the LaMotte newsroom almost three decades earlier.

"Somebody get me UPI up in Chicago," demanded Randolph, who was the first publisher/executive editor in Cratty's career and the very last individual he could recall filling those two chairs with the same rear-end.

He was also averse to handling the mundane functions required in actually getting someone on the telephone and he forbid being called anything other than "Mr. Randolph."

When he made a call, Cratty or somebody else in the office had to ring the number and get someone on the line.

"I've got a four-year-old granddaughter who could write a better lead," added Mr. Randolph, who had never uttered a subdued word in his life.

"Hello, this UPI's state desk?" he asked over the phone, once Chicago got on the line. "What imbecile you guys got covering the statehouse these days?

"Well, this lightweight just sent me a story, which I would assume somebody on your desk cleared, that I'd stick up the ass of any reporter of mine who turned it out."

When you were called into Mr. Randolph's office, it was always a good practice to say your goodbyes and dictate your last will and testament to fellow staff members as you made your way across the eerily silent newsroom. Nobody had the guts to look at you in the eye as you made that dead man's walk.

Mr. Randolph didn't seem to be a very understanding boss. You picked it up as he laid it down, or you didn't pick it up at all and you were out the front door. He could cut you to pieces using his tongue as a copy knife and could care less who else in the building or walking by on the street out front could hear your dying throes.

But Mr. Randolph knew everything there was to know about the newspaper business. And anyone who lasted more than a week working for the crusty old son of a bitch learned more about the business than they could pick up in a year under another boss or four years in a college journalism class.

Now the front offices of newspapers from coast to coast are stocked with guys with slicked back hair and bad ties, who don't know their "butts from page six," as Mr. Randolph used to put it.

All they know is debt load and how to slash expenses. And they haven't the slightest compunction about how and just what they have to cut to the bone to accomplish their goal.

But the one thing they have no understanding of at all is journalism.

Cratty used to believe in that old saw about "You go to war as a boy and come back a man!"

That is until he came back himself. Now he was sure that you might have gone as a "boy," but you came back a fool.

And it was usually as a fool who was certain he was both 10-feet tall and bulletproof.

That was the story of his life, at least the last quarter century or so of it.

He'd returned from 'Nam absolutely sure he would live forever. Not only live forever but have the entire world by the ass as his plaything.

That was the reason for three failed marriages and God knows how many relationships, 10 newspapers in the last two-plus decades, and a distinct inability to conform to the usual pecking order that amounts to survival in the working world.

It cost him dearly, but that was another of those things it'd take the rest of his life to come to terms with.

It was a line item in a city budget from a few years before his arrival at the Warren Reporter News in 1993.

The Warren City Council had replaced the windows at City Hall. It was a bill in the neighborhood of $80,000.

Evidently, the good citizens had caught a break on the price because one of the members of the council was, as luck would have it, a local building contractor.

However, it seems that almost $12,000 of the price was, in fact, the councilman's commission on the deal. And remarkably, it was an open secret at City Hall. Although a sitting member of the council could not legally benefit from such an arrangement, the power structure, such as it was, had no problem letting this slip by.

Cratty couldn't quite recall how the matter, years after the fact, had come to his attention, but he wasted little time bringing it to everybody else's. He spent two columns a month, the ones preceding every bi-weekly council meeting for the next few months, telling the local builder (who was no longer on the council but still doing business in the community) to bring his checkbook to the council chambers.

Come to think of it, the guy never did pay up, but there's no doubt he kept a considerably lower profile and suffered somewhat of a business slowdown in town for some time after that.

As was always the case, the builder and his many friends directed their anger toward the messenger, more concerned with their and the city's image than the misdeed.

But the contractor was the first and as it turned out the only miscreant that got off scot-free during Cratty's tenure at the Reporter News.

And that minor matter was one of the least explosive items to come out of Cratty's computer in just over two years at Warren.

Another member of the council thought it proper to store his outdoor plant life on the upper floor of City Hall each winter sans reimbursement to city coffers. That probably would have been OK had the same privilege been offered to the rest of the citizenry – as northern Illinois can cause a lot of damage to the floral life between November and March – but it was not.

The same councilman, who was a pharmacist by trade, was also pushing the city-owned hospital to employ him on a full-time basis to handle such chores for the medical facility. The problem was that his advances were rejected by hospital staff, probably owing to the trivial matter of a state slap on the hands for issuing medications minus prescriptions.

The pharmacist must have learned his job search approach from the town's mayor, who in addition to a full-time state job, also just happened to be employed by the local city-owned hospital's primary ambulance provider.

Now, Warren was a town with a population of some 11,000. So, it's easy to see that someone in Cratty's position might wind up with a less than favorable view of human nature, especially when it came to small town politicians. It was enough to give one a skewed outlook of anyplace where more than a handful of people gather together for the community.

Livingstone was a town about the same size as Warren, and like Warren was the rural county seat.

During his Livingstone stint, which preceded his tenure at Warren, Cratty's impression of local politics and business types was just as disconcerting.

As the sports editor in his initial stint at Livingstone, Cratty came across many items that would – like many later in his career – help stir the pot.

And it's just like magic how these kinds of tales always lead to a virtual landslide of misadventures.

Stirring the shit in Viet Nam was, if not an honorable profession, certainly a necessary one. Armies throughout time have wrestled with the fact that soldiers need to both eat and shit. And toward that end, it only took several thousand years for the military geniuses concerned to discover that keeping the eating part separate from the shitting was a healthy idea. There is no telling how many military campaigns probably failed due to the many deadly diseases involved in lax fecal hygiene.

In 'Nam, the job of shit-stirrer served both as a sanitary duty and handy punishment.

The process consisted of cutting a 55-gallon drum in half and placing the rounded containers under a raised platform known as a latrine. The Army developed the structure over a long history of field operations. It kept the physical necessities confined to a spot away from the troops' living and eating areas and thereby reduced the health problems caused by following the old bear shit in the woods' method.

By a wide margin, most of the deaths suffered by Americans on both sides of the Civil War were the result of disease. Any time you bring a large number of men, especially those from rural settings, where they're less likely to have been exposed to crowded living conditions together to build an army, there is a high propensity for the spread of disease.

And handling the residuals of defecation was first on the list of military necessities.

It is an interesting historical footnote that the vaunted German Afrika Corps was greatly handicapped during the protracted battles in North Africa in World War II due to its lack of field hygiene. In fact, some have attributed the eventual British victory in the campaign in part to the fact that the Germans were virtually decimated by disease because they didn't know how to properly separate the consumption of food and its biological elimination.

But the most recent practice of combating this situation also necessitates the disposal of the accumulated waste material, which required an individual, usually a miscreant private – to take a long rod and a 5-gallon can of diesel fuel to accomplish the chore.

The fuel was poured in, and once a fire got going, the object of the exercise was to stir the contents until the solid matter was burned away.

The funniest story about the practice Cratty ever heard was about a guy called "Weed," who was once hard at work stirring said shit when the battalion's Top Shirt (first sergeant) happened along and asked what he was up to. Well, Weed didn't hesitate to inform Top that he was trying his best to build himself a sergeant and just couldn't seem to "find enough shit."

Of course, the quip earned Weed another day or two on the detail, but it also loomed large in his eventual legend in the outfit.

Cratty was certainly starting to fall out of love with the newspaper business by about his third decade in it.

He'd climbed in at the high-water mark, in the early 1970s, when Woodward and Bernstein and Watergate were the headlines. But anybody who saw that as the start of a bright future for journalism would be sadly disappointed by what followed.

The powers that be in all segments of American society, those who were the natural targets of "investigative journalism," simply had to find a way to counter the power of the pen.

The tumult of the 1960s also seemed to put a scare into both the political and business elite, as demonstrated by a very famous memo written by future Supreme Court Justice Lewis Powell. After watching the youth of the nation, its so-called press enablers and the civil rights movement literally take America by the throat, out of one war and snatch a president from the heights of political power, those in charge panicked.

So, they just created a whole new game.

Powell's missive, written in 1971 suggested that anti-capitalist forces in the country were in open revolt against the free enterprise system, as clearly demonstrated by the events of the previous decade.

The resulting objective was to blunt the truth with obfuscation, outright suppression and an assault, legal and otherwise on the messenger. If you couldn't change the facts, then you had to change the way they were perceived and disparage those dispensing them.

It was all too easy, thanks to print media's sudden love affair with advertising's profits. Thus, the advent of media based on profit instead of readership, it became easier to please the guy paying most of the bills than those availing themselves of the daily paper.

Then, newspapers totally capitulated, pushing out publishers who were real journalists and replacing them with those who were providing the profits. Newspapers had finally begun abdicating their integral role, furthering a free and open democratic society, for one as the moneychangers in the temple.

Those with the most money and stature in the community, in other words, those with the most to lose from the prying eyes of the press, were then in a position to actually affect those prying eyes.

Now none of this probably has much of an effect on the country's leading print publications, who with the help of nationwide coverage and the highest journalistic credentials and standards have insulated themselves and their newsrooms from this sort of thing.

But the majority of newspapers, both daily and weekly, in America are not insulated or protected. And these publications are where the practice of journalism's rubber really meets the road for the overwhelming number of U.S. citizens.

It used to be the object of the exercise to build readership and thus attract the ad revenue by pointing out the number of potential customers that a business could reach.

But advertisers, sitting atop the economic hierarchy of any community, aren't big on the controversy. It's bad for business, especially their business.

Meanwhile, readers were no longer part of the equation.

And since the business community is too often the target of bad press and intertwined with local government, the power wielded by the advertisers served to kill two birds with the one proverbial stoning.

It's much easier to simply replace the pointed message with something a little more peaceful. Then, after years of seeing the local communities' blemishes glossed over or dismissed, the readers figured out the scam. They stopped trusting the messenger and decided they didn't need to have newspapers tell them anything.

That led to an emphasis on bright color, more white space, and "human interest" stories. But unfortunately for publications, the only readers attracted to those pieces were the subjects of the printed item and their immediate family and friends. That certainly limited the audience.

Any time a higher percentage of the local community knows more about what's going on than the population of your newsroom, you've already lost the battle.

Thus, once the readers jumped ship because the paper was no longer telling them what they needed to know, the advertising department was left with a dwindling product, and an even faster decline in the revenue attached to it.

Enter the internet. Newspaper executives, already comprised entirely of ad reps and circulation types, went off the rails with an idea of giving everything away online, thrilled at the possibility of cornering the next generation of ad revenue.

When they finally figured out there was very little to be gained in that endeavor, unless you could reach millions of potential consumers, they discovered shilling for the new ad money was folly.

Then, some circulation genius came up with the brilliant idea of installing "pay walls" and online subscriptions. Ten to 15 years after they'd already given the content away for free, that ship had sailed.

Far too late the bean counters realized that the news they'd already spent time, talent, and treasure to gather indeed had a real value. However, they'd pissed away the people who were once willing to pay you for it.

By then the readership base they had worked more than a century to build was gone. That left little chance of ever getting it back.

You also can't preserve your credibility with the reader by trying to copy TV and tell people what you think they want to know.

That's not what people want to read. Cratty proved at more than a couple of publications that keeping them up to speed on what they, and the rest of the community, needed to know solves the readership problem.

A TV talking head uses a total of 30 seconds to tell a story that could only begin to be spelt out in nothing short of 20 inches. Cratty never came across a broadcast news story that offered much more than what you could fit in a one-column headline. And then, in the cable news era broadcasters simply started confiscating, either by outright theft or on-air contributions, the information being compiled in the nation's leading newsrooms.

Cratty once wrote a column, after some stiff objections from his publisher, telling his readers that "it's not my job to sell you this newspaper."

In fact, Cratty opined that it was his job instead to make you want to "steal it."

"I'm not in the business of selling this paper or the advertising within. My lot in life is, to the best of my ability, to get you to read it. I don't care if that's done at the kitchen table, by putting change in a box or pawing over somebody else's discarded scraps. If you're reading, I've done my job. Everything else means squat."

And he proved it time and time again.

While at Livingstone, Cratty's venture into county politics and the resulting upending of the sheriff's race was an excellent example of his philosophy.

At the wake held by the losing candidate on election night, close to 100 in attendance vowed to cancel their subscriptions to the Livingstone Reader. However, in the weeks that followed, the single copy sales for the publication more than tripled, leaving the controversial scribe to point out the simple fact that his employer was making twice the profit with just a fraction of the effort.

"People will read good, well-sourced hard news," Cratty once told a college class at State. "In fact, I've found that those on the receiving end of such journalistic efforts are the most addicted readers!"

When he was about to leave northern New Mexico in early fall of 1999, Cratty hooked up by phone with his 'Nam platoon sergeant, "Bill" Davis. The crusty former E-7 was back home in southwestern Ohio.

That led to reuniting a relationship that would last decades.

The two reconnected for real at a division reunion at Fort Campbell in about 2000.

After leaving New Mexico, Cratty was sidelined for the next three months trying to get back into the business. That's when Delaware called and put him back in a newsroom – his last – and it would be his professional home for the next almost 16 years.

His farewell in the Southwest was almost the exact opposite of any other desk he exited in his career. In fact, he would remove himself from the New Mexico position despite and not because of his penchant for stirring the shit.

His final offering on the editorial page was a goodbye piece telling his readers, both Indian and white, that he would not continue to be the personal bludgeon of the maniac in the publisher's office.

When the wingnut, who was easily the most unhinged boss of his career, finally read the piece, he stormed out to the editor's desk and informed Cratty that from now on, he'd have to run columns past the front office before publication.

"Obviously, you failed to read the entire piece," Cratty explained to his enraged boss. "That was my last column for this paper. I have already given two weeks' notice to your father (CEO)."

The publisher's comeback was to banish Cratty to the mailroom for those last two weeks.

"I've worked the mailroom before, and I'm gonna be the highest paid bundle wrapper you've ever had in this place."

The president of the family-owned operation spared Cratty what he might have thought was the humiliation of stacking bundles in the circulation department by insisting he keeps his desk in the newsroom for the final 10 days on the job.

So, despite his editorial talents, which were far from diminished by the better part of 30 years in the business, Cratty was able to recognize when his controversial talents were being misused.

6. "Car 54, Where Are You...?"

"We just can't seem to attract readers," one of Cratty's publishers, ounce groused. "People want more color, white space, and catchy graphics. We need to give the reader more of what he wants, because obviously, he's tuned us out."

He'd always counter with, "I never ever wrote anything with a reader in mind!

"Actually, I don't know nor care what the reader wants," he'd quickly counter.

Of course, this was akin to blasphemy, and surely anyone who espoused such heretical thought should be burned at the stake.

But Cratty was certain that what the proverbial reader really wanted was the truth, straight up and unvarnished. The public depends, or at least used to depend on the news media to open all the windows and doors. They want to be told what they need to know, not lulled to sleep with the cute and entertaining bits about school plays, lunches, business openings and the occasional mother duck trying to lead her brood through traffic or the extrication of cats from trees.

He was convinced in his approach that if you give people something worth reading, they'll respond and proved it over the years.

However, it would take 13 different newspapers before Cratty would finally lay down his quill. And despite his constant complaining about over edited and nitpicked pieces, it wouldn't be that issue that would finally lead to his newsroom exit.

He discovered that the once thrilling beginning portended by the excitement of the early 1970s – when he was getting started and Watergate captivated the nation – was indeed the high-water mark of the business. From there, the wave so eloquently depicted by Dr. Hunter Thompson once again slipped back into the sea.

First came the bean counters, glorified paperboys in suits, ensconced in the biggest offices usually one flight below the newsroom. That way, in case of fire you could save the brain trust. They always knew they could find enough kids fresh out of college to fill the spaces between the ads for $12,000 per year.

Then they came for the guardians of the art, those crusty old fringe types dedicated to finding that most elusive of commodities – The Truth.

They had to go because firstly, they were the biggest drag on the bottom line, and secondly, they were people the bookkeepers couldn't understand or even talk with. Cratty recalled an early career prediction that if those in charge could have found one of their newfangled computers that could cover and then produce a passable story on its own, they would opt for the devices because the front office wouldn't have to either figure out their wage/benefits nor have to actually deal with obstinate human beings.

It happened after a month or two of pounding on the local Republican Party's candidate for sheriff. As editor at the Livingstone Reader, Cratty had blasted the upstart sheriff's detective for a vendetta he'd had with another member of the department, which like most organizations had an "in" and "out" group.

Cratty had always said that his professional prowess depended on just that trait in human nature.

"If you've got a connection on both sides of the battling power base in any organization," he'd try to explain to up and coming scribes, "you'd be surprised just how close that could put you to the truth in any perceived conflict."

In Livingstone's political power base, which consisted of GOP one-party rule, Cratty found just such a rift. That led to one of the biggest stories of his few years in east-central Illinois. It also proved another tenant of Cratty's professional approach, all you need is to turn over that first piece of information, and the tips never end.

Seems a deputy – one of the close associates of the party's pick for sheriff – had taken a fugitive out of state a couple a hundred miles from Livingstone. He'd stayed overnight after depositing his package, and when he woke up the next morning, he'd misplaced a county squad car stocked with weapons and all the rest of its regular accoutrements.

He reported what he believed was the theft of the car to local police, who quickly discovered that the deputy must have forgotten where he parked the vehicle in all the obviously inebriated celebrations of the night before.

Yes, the County-Mounty had gone on a bit of a toot with the help of a female acquaintance imported from Livingstone and simply left the squad parked two miles from the hotel he supposedly spent the night in.

Having already established a relationship with the "out" delegation at the sheriff's department, Cratty's phone rang bright and early the morning of the embarrassing incident. Thanks to that tip, that same afternoon's front-page hitting doorsteps greeted readers with a massive headline and the hilarious tale of "Car 54, where are you…?"

Once the readers of any newspaper know that the power of the press is as much if not more theirs as it is for those in office, they soon discover it could easily open doors to many of any town's secrets.

"People will read it, if you give them something to read," Cratty's mantra would begin. "And, colors, graphics, and strategic white space are certainly not the answer.

"The best newspapers in the industry are the worst looking rags on the rack. Take the New York Times, Whiteout the masthead and put it next to a stack of papers from everywhere on the map, and one of your graphic designer types wouldn't give it a second look. The finest examples of the art have absolutely nothing to do with layout.

"I always wrote for the guy at the next desk," Cratty constantly preached, "not for Joe Blow on the street. If I could sell it at the next desk, I wasn't the least bit worried about what the general public thought."

Early in his career, Cratty would always bounce story ideas and/or leads off others in the newsroom. However, toward and after the new millennium, stories were gathered in silence someplace outside a newsroom, and except for the quiet keystrokes on a computer somewhere off in the distance, the noise was not only kept at a minimum but was too often forbidden.

"If you read your lead graph to the guy at the next desk and you can do so without stumbling over it, so could the guy sitting at his kitchen table," Cratty would tell the rookies, who were constantly being warned about making too much noise in the newsroom. The problem was they weren't being given enough time to learn their craft. They were simply turned loose with all the crap they learned in a lecture hall, where you could hear a pin drop but not much in the way of practical application.

He came home from a usual late Friday night stretch on the copy desk in Delaware and saw the light flashing on the answering machine. It was DeBonis asking Cratty to call him at home – a trailer in Leavenworth, Kan.

He didn't sound well, but then he never really did, between several decades of drug and alcohol abuse added to a smoking habit that was up to two and three packs a day, DeBonis had pushed his already frail body to the limit. He never weighed more than 140 pounds soaking wet, and when they finally got together after decades up in Leavenworth in about 2005, DeBonis was under driving restrictions from one of several DUI convictions that required him to blow into a breathalyzer to start his second-hand pick-up and to keep it going every 15 minutes.

It was after 1 a.m. when Cratty finally got the message. So, he decided to wait till morning to return the call.

That would be a mistake.

The two spent quite a bit of time catching up, both on the phone and in person, since reconnecting.

But the friendship ran out of time that night.

Before Cratty could get to the phone that Saturday morning, his Facebook page was already buzzing about the fact that DeBonis had passed away in his sleep sometime Friday night or earlier that morning.

Then a person Cratty had met on one of his treks to Leavenworth – one of the hangers-on who found it much too easy to take advantage of the alcoholic – called and broke the news.

That was a perfect ending to his relationship with DeBonis, someone he thought the world of but whose lifestyle had put him off for its "there but for the grace of God" similarity to his own.

He couldn't wait to see his friend, and then five minutes after arriving, he couldn't wait to leave. He couldn't quite put a finger on it, but all the cigarette smoke hanging in the air and the empty vodka bottles probably had a lot to do with it.

He found that he could never bring himself to eat at DeBonis' apartment, a rent-reduced disabled veterans' complex in Leavenworth, where one of the country's biggest veterans' medical facilities was located. DeBonis was on 100% disability, between PTSD and the addictions. Cratty couldn't quite get over feeling he was staring at himself in a mirror save for the fact that his first marriage and two daughters seemed to be the major redeeming difference.

He was convinced that his daughters, and the fact that their mother was left to raise them back in Iowa, were the only things that kept him from a drug-fueled haze and needing to blow into a breathalyzer to drive a car. That and the newspaper business.

DeBonis also had a couple of kids, neither one of which, as he would too often relate, he could recognize if they passed on the street.

It was the hard-living lifestyle after his friend's return from 'Nam that strained his marriage to the breaking point, just like it had Cratty's first.

Cratty had almost sat his friend down to try to intervene the last time they were together in Kansas, just a few short weeks before DeBonis passed away. In fact, DeBonis' twin sister had called while he was there and asked if he'd stay long enough to help her confront him about his deteriorating health and drinking.

But, as it always was on those trips, Cratty couldn't wait to get back to Iowa. That was just one more thing that would haunt him about his friend's death for the rest of his life.

Cratty pulled back from trying to tell the best friend he had in 'Nam how to live his life. Perhaps it was the thin line between that life and his own, or the fact that he was certain his friend was as immune to preaching as he'd always been.

And Cratty would really be the last one to talk.

As things would turn out, Cratty had made something of an impact on DeBonis after all. On one of his trips to the K.C. area, Cratty brought his oldest grandson to a Royals game. They stayed overnight in the Leavenworth apartment, and his grandson spent the next day's trip back to Iowa violently ill from all the cigarette smoke in the air.

A week or so later, DeBonis gave up smoking cold turkey. It was about the only thing Cratty could say about the more than 40-year friendship that he could offer as his positive contribution. That and the fact he truly loved the guy.

Here was a man with a quick-witted sense of humor and an absolute loyalty that transcended anything on this earth. And despite the fact that the pair couldn't seem to find a single topic to agree on, they positively enjoyed every word of the debate.

"You know, Jake, you're the only liberal I've ever been able to enjoy talking to," DeBonis offered during one particular discussion. "In fact, I'd rather talk politics with you than anybody else in this world."

Cratty was certain there would never be another human being he'd ever known that he'd admire or love more than DeBonis. Thankfully, he got a chance to tell him that between his final visit to Kansas and the man's death.

DeBonis' sister told Cratty that her brother considered him the best friend he had in the world sometime before he died. She added that this was the single greatest thing he'd taken from the reunion that restarted too many decades too late.

However, that did little to ease the pain of all those times Cratty couldn't wait to leave his friend whenever they were together.

"Wanted: A managing editor for a 19,000 plus, six-day-a-week daily in northwestern New Mexico. Send an updated resume, writing and layout samples and salary requirements."

He absolutely hated this part of the process. Pull out the old resume, which by now was two years too old and as much as 35 pounds too heavy.

When he'd moved to Michigan, he was going through his third, and he hoped final divorce.

It wasn't a nasty split, but it was enough of an unpleasant experience that he didn't want to go through it again.

Beth was a wonderful person, just not a person Cratty was really in love with. In the end, he couldn't even remember just how he felt when they'd gotten married four years earlier.

He remembered loving Catrina, his first wife, the mother of his two children. Actually, in a very real sense, Cratty still loved Catrina even though the final years and breakup were among the worst of his life.

Catrina was probably the best decision Cratty made relationship-wise. And if he hadn't had his big head already halfway up his own ass back then, he'd have handled it much better for everyone involved.

And Cat filing for divorce 12 years later was probably the best of her life. But without her and those two girls, Cratty hated to think just how dismal an existence he might have had, not unlike DeBonis.

He did remember that the breakup of his first marriage was the worst year of his life. Much worse even than he remembered his year in Viet Nam.

His second marriage, the fastest 15 months of his life, ended with barely a ripple. Sarah, a girl nearly 14 years younger, had married him and moved down to Texas, and then he just seemed to drift away. It was like he was walking in his sleep. However, much of the split had to do with how his daughters reacted to the marriage. It was too much to ask of her – being just nine years older than his oldest – and the girls, who were left 900 miles from their father and more than a little worried about his loyalty as well.

When he woke up, she'd moved back to Illinois, and he started that part of his life he remembered as being completely numb.

He felt little if anything at all. He remembered going for almost two years back in the 1980s without any female contact whatsoever, except those of his two daughters, mother and sister.

So, now he was starting all over once again. He'd left Warren after two years at the local newspaper and left Beth all in one move, and now he was off on another search for a new job and probably a completely new life, going from Michigan to god knows where.

A new Sarah in his life was of major help for Cratty, who'd met the woman with two grown sons while serving at Livingstone. They would marry a couple of years later, and the arrangement, as strange as some might think it, would stick.

The reasons he'd left Warren weren't a whole lot, unlike the reasons he was leaving Michigan.

While there was a marriage (his third) to disassemble, he'd once again worked himself into one of those situations only Cratty could manufacture.

Two years earlier, the election campaign from hell had erupted in Warren, and Cratty found himself right in the middle, as usual. It wasn't that he really minded being at the center of the storm. Come to think of it, it was a spot he dearly enjoyed.

It was just that it got so goddamned personal, so fucking fast.

In the end, even though it didn't help, the city fathers – an administration of local petty politicians, who were, in reality, a few medium-sized fish in nothing bigger than a mud puddle – had aimed the harshest broadsides of their campaign at Cratty. And he wasn't even on the ballot.

The final straw for Cratty, or at least that's what he told himself, came when they called and badgered his stepdaughter Beth's youngest – he'd already moved out of Beth's home – on the phone in an attempt to find his new phone number and address.

"Don't let Pat Cratty tell us how to run our city," blared one of the radio ads. "Let's send a message to Pat Cratty and those other slanderers down at the Warren Reporter News," was another.

Hell, he'd have simply pulled up stakes for half the money they wasted on such crap, he once joked. "But nobody ever thought to just offer me a bribe!"

It was a stormy two years at Warren, just like the last couple here in Michigan.

But looking back on it, he had to smile just a little. They'd been such easy prey when he thought about it.

The guy who was Warren mayor, a former city policeman/city councilman/state employee, was a childish, ill-tempered twit.

He'd been dismissed from the town's police force several years earlier for, among other things, pulling his service revolver on an assistant state's attorney who had made fun of his hat. There were other notable instances of erratic behavior in his law enforcement career, but suffice it to say he'd been fired.

He even went to court in an attempt to regain his position but had been turned down for what the appellate court called "behavior that was a threat to the community."

Yeah, this guy was a gem.

Cratty had no idea how he'd ended up winning the highest executive office in the town of 11,000.

And he evidently spent much of his official time "getting even" for having been dismissed.

Within days of being sworn in, he named a former friend he'd had on the force – his only pal there apparently – more than a decade earlier as police chief. Of course, he had to promote the guy over a raft of more qualified officers, bumping him up from little more than street patrolman. But he accomplished the feat.

However, that was a couple of years before Cratty got to town.

One of Cratty's first columns, after he arrived, was a recounting of the unpleasantness that had accompanied the mayor's dismissal years before. The new editor was amazed that something that was such common knowledge came as such a bombshell.

It took several months for the mayor to come down from that blow-up, and there was a strong rumor that one of his buddies had to go to the mayor's office and take a handgun out of his desk for fear he'd give a repeat performance of the stunt he pulled with the assistant state's attorney, only this time in the local newspaper office.

But things didn't get that wild. At least not just yet.

The local hospital was under municipal control, and it just so happened that the city and county's ambulance contract was in the hands of one of the mayor's friends. And the potential for a conflict of interest didn't end there, as the friend also gave him a job driving emergency vehicles. The mayor made a few thousand dollars a year from part-time employment with the ambulance service that had its only major contract with the city-owned and operated hospital.

It was the most fertile field Cratty had ever had the good luck or misfortune to be set down in to that stage of his career. And the mayor's famous temper tantrums, conflicts of interest and other erratic behavior proved only the tip of the iceberg.

There was seldom a two-week period that went by that some other major local story or other wasn't breaking.

There was the local cop who, while transporting a suspect in a bar fight in the back seat of his cruiser, had to divert to the hospital because the gun the officer failed to find in the pants of his passenger went off while he was trying to shake it loose and kick it under the car's seat. The wound was almost fatal as the bullet wound up severing an artery.

Well, suffice it to say Cratty had a field day as editor of the community's paper, and as it turned out the mayor's seeming lock on the City Hall front door went from a cinch to a no holds barred battle within a matter of months.

Within weeks of the spring election, another scandal hit the front-page.

The city clerk, who had swept into office with the mayor four years earlier and also was considered a shoe-in for re-election, was found to have been somewhat less than competent in her handling of city finances.

The town's water and sewer receipts were estimated to be a couple a thousand dollars short, with much of it written off. There was not even much of a system to shut off the services of those who were grossly in arrears.

And even the auditing firm, called in to look at the books – which took an extra three months to complete because of the clerk's ragged bookkeeping practices – was scathing in its appraisal of the situation.

But the clincher came when someone stole a couple of thousand dollars in water/sewer-bill receipts, and the city clerk, who had all but dismantled the computer system of her predecessor, had no way of knowing the funds were gone until someone who'd paid fees called four months later to find out why the check had never cleared the bank. Only then did the woman discover the missing money, and her chance at another four years in the office went down the drain as well.

Her fate was tied to the mayor, and a relentless battering of both and others in the local paper took its toll. And the candidates, who looked to have no real opposition just six months earlier, were suddenly in a fight for their political lives.

As is the way in most such circumstances, cockroaches preferred the lights out and figured the best way to turn off the switch was in discrediting Cratty.

The radio ads began two months before the race. Another campaign was aimed at newspaper ads directed at Cratty in his hometown paper, which was situated just a few miles east of Warren, where he resided.

"I'll be leaving as soon after Election Day as I can find some place to land," Cratty told the Warren publisher three weeks before the balloting.

"Look, Pat, all this will blow over," countered his boss, trying desperately to calm his obviously infuriated editor.

"These people will get re-elected and then they'll forget all this."

Cratty shrugged, discovering that his publisher had no more of a feel for the local political pulse than he had for editorial policy and content.

"No! They're not going to win this election and they are definitely not going to ever forget this."

Election Day came, and the mayor was swept out of office along with the city clerk, as well as at least one of the four members of the City Council seeking re-election.

About the only thing that seemed to be going Cratty's way as he looked for a new job after Indiana City was a new Sarah. He soon forgot about promising himself his third marriage was his last. Just before the blow-up between him and the new publisher, Cratty asked her to marry him. Neither of them realized at the time they'd have to endure almost another year of separation before they were married – the fourth for each.

They'd met shortly after Cratty arrived at Livingstone in early 1991. She was the Reader's bookkeeper and he was first the sports editor and then executive editor at the paper, after spending almost a year at a weekly chain headquartered about 16 miles from Livingstone on the south edge of the county.

Before they would finally marry, in May of 1999, Cratty would spend almost four years married to Beth – two of those at Warren.

"I'm calling about the managing editor's job," said Cratty, a little hesitant over the telephone. He always hated calling people cold about a job. And it was the first and last time he'd ask about a position sight unseen.

You never really knew what these situations were going to lead to, and you always hung on every word, each inflection, trying to read much more into it than there probably was.

"Why, yes," answered the voice on the other end, who was, as far as Cratty could tell, close in age to himself. The guy was the current executive editor and said that he needed somebody "yesterday." He also hinted that the working conditions were a bit unconventional and that he was trying to whip a rather young and inexperienced staff into shape in a community situated in the middle of the Navajo Nation, the largest Indian reservation in the world.

"Are you looking for a position?" asked the guy, putting Cratty a little more at ease.

He liked the guy's voice, and the way he put the inquiry seemed to take a lot of the tension out of the conversation. "Yes, I am," Cratty came back, not wanting to let the banter drag. "In fact, I needed a job yesterday.

"I'd really like to find a new home," he continued, knowing that the comment sounded strange coming from someone who couldn't really remember ever having one.

7. Crazy Days

It was certainly a mistake to take the first job he was offered when Cratty made his decision to leave Michigan, but it was a mistake he didn't feel the full force of for almost a year.

"I needed a city editor a month ago," said the voice on the other end of the phone in New Mexico.

"You don't know me, and all I know of you is the stuff you sent me in an email," added the executive editor of the Dessert News, a 20,000 circulation, six-day-a-week p.m. newspaper serving the white and Indian community along the southeastern Four Corners area of the New Mexico-Arizona border region.

It would end up, after some of the weirdest months of his entire career, with Cratty as the executive editor, working for the craziest motherfucker he'd ever known. This guy was so nuts that Cratty would be remembered as the leveling influence in the building.

"I've accepted the No. 2 job at a daily in northwest New Mexico," said Cratty as he stuck his head into Bird's office. It was just behind his desk in the middle of the newsroom, which was little more than a wide-open warehouse with a high drop ceiling.

"Don't suppose I could get ya' to change your mind," said Bird quickly, trying to at least drag Cratty in and engage in one of their usual long-winded conversations.

"Howard, you know better than that," said Cratty, trying to extricate himself as fast as he could to spare any hard feelings. "I've worn out my welcome here. We both know that."

He liked it along the shoreline, one hell of a lot more than he ever thought he would. He also liked Bird, a guy of his generation and like-minded approach to newspapering.

Bird's only problem was that he'd already given up the ghost and was too busy just trying to hang on to the job to fight the good fight in the newsroom.

Cratty had developed a loyal following, and his regular targets were in a constant state of discomfort and in great supply.

"You know, one of these days somebody's gonna try and silence you once and for all," his youngest daughter had once half-heartedly warned. It was one of those jokes that has just enough truth to it to keep everybody from laughing out loud.

Since reaching the shores of Lake Michigan, he'd almost reinvented himself, losing 40 to 45 pounds and pushing his running back up to the 30-miles-per-week average. There was a period, back in Illinois when he and Beth were still together, when he'd ballooned to 220 pounds and was practically sedentary, reducing his running to barely five miles per week, with almost all of that confined to a treadmill at the local YMCA.

So, he'd made up his mind upon arriving in Michigan to get back into running and drop all the extra weight.

And he'd accomplished that goal as well as finding a real relationship with Sarah No. 2.

He was back down to about 175 pounds and logged six to seven miles five days a week religiously.

Viet Nam was a very touchy subject for Cratty, especially those years between his return from the war and about 1980. It was a topic he didn't discuss himself and wouldn't sit around listening to somebody else talk about either.

Mostly, that was because when he'd arrived back home from 'Nam, the country he returned to was also in turmoil over the war itself. By that time the label "Baby Killers" had long since replaced "America, love it or leave it."

At that point, he told himself, "If you weren't there, you don't know. And if you were, there's nothing I can tell ya."

But then that was quite a while back as he saw it all now. So far back it seemed like someone else's life.

As the years stretched into decades since his overseas stint, Cratty felt a war going on inside of himself.

As the 1970s unfolded, he was so damned sure that all the ideals that propelled him to the other side of the world and that war were the highest forms of patriotism on the altar of American hero worship. He was proud of what he'd done over there and really resented his father's downgrading it all when he first came back.

Then, as the '70s ended, he felt himself growing angrier and angrier. And he had no idea why.

At first, he thought it was the disinterest of the succeeding generation.

"They had nothing to do with the war, and they could give a good goddamn about any of us who risked our asses."

As the '80s dawned, along with Delayed Stress Syndrome – a malady he never thought he believed in – he wasn't near as sure anymore.

He kept getting madder, and he started seeing it in the way he practiced his profession.

Viet Nam was certainly something that was never very far from his mind. And why should it be? It was, as he saw it at least, the defining moment of his life.

As Cratty would eventually discover, much too late in life to be of any real help, just how empty that thought was, and regret ever having believed it in the first place.

He'd changed markedly in that year between mid-1965 and mid-1966. And it was most certainly his adventure in Southeast Asia that was the cause of his suddenly unsettled emotional state three decades after the fact. It controlled almost his every thought that's for sure and was the filter through which he experienced every single moment since.

And heaven knows he was in possession of one of the most unsettled emotional states around. Oh, he wasn't volatile enough to be really dangerous, or anything like that. But there was always some small shred of doubt in the minds of many others.

In the early 1990s, he started sporting long hair, something he'd always wanted to do his entire life, or at least that portion of his life since he'd become cognizant of such affectations. Even as a kid he loved long hair, with the only difference being that now he no longer used a quart of Brylcreem he needed to give himself a pompadour and "duck's ass" like when he was a teenie-bopper in pegged pants and a T-shirt.

"Left it a little long there on the sides, didn't ya' Jake?" his old man would ask as he sat facing his eldest situated in the barber's chair.

Every other Saturday of his pre-teen life as a kid he'd spent trailing his father down North Street for a regular appointment at Al's.

His father was determined that his oldest boy wasn't going to look like one of those juvenile delinquent ragamuffins who stood on street corners trying to look cool in the latter 1950s and early '60s.

And his first-born son was bound and determined to look like nothing else.

"I don't want to see any headlines in my paper with the word 'Homicide,'" the New Mexico publisher announced soon after Cratty's arrival in late 1998. "Nobody understands that word, and murder looks a lot better in a headline."

As it turned out, the publisher had absolutely no understanding of "that word" himself.

The guy was the son of the man who'd purchased the paper many years earlier and who still served as the publication's president. The problem was that he'd long since surrendered any real control of the paper to his son, who was a volatile, bi-polar maniac who thought he had some grasp of the newspaper business.

He didn't, and proved it every time he opened his shit-filled mouth.

"We use words like 'murder' in my paper," the publisher would insist. And try as one might, it did no good to explain to him there might have been a legal difference involved.

But, as Cratty would soon learn, that was one of his more rational beliefs.

Unlike most of the other publishers, Cratty had served under over the past 20 plus years or so, his new boss was not a "bean counter." Hell, Cratty wouldn't be surprised to find the idiot couldn't count to 10.

He didn't hail from the distribution side of the business and had absolutely no understanding of journalism, which made him an even bigger threat as far as Cratty was concerned.

Once he'd moved into the top spot on the staff, Cratty discovered that his primary duty was to stand squarely between his young staff and the raging maniac in the publisher's office.

"P.J., you're going to want to talk to that intern," Cratty's new wife, visiting from Illinois sometime in August, greeted him as he exited a meeting in which he'd dressed down another loose cannon member of the staff behind closed doors.

Cratty turned to see a 19-year-old in tears and the rest of the newsroom practically hiding under their desks. Seems the publisher had used Cratty's brief absence from the newsroom to go on an insane rant over a puff piece written by the summer intern – an SMU student – about the community's hospital board president.

That was his modus operandi. He'd wait for Cratty to be out of the office or out of earshot and then pounce on members of the newsroom staff too scared to fight back.

He knew Cratty would fight back and wasn't too sure things wouldn't get downright physical before it ended.

According to Mrs. Cratty, who witnessed the verbal assault, the bullying asshole of a publisher had stormed through the newsroom shouting about what he referred to as "this shit article" about the "whore" who was serving as the hospital board president.

The publisher had some very obnoxious opinions regarding certain social elites and most of the others in town. And he was not too shy when it came to spouting off about the same people in both private and public settings.

Evidently, there wasn't anyone among the community's elite that the publisher hadn't either verbally assaulted or who had returned the favor.

He once got into a fistfight with the town's mayor just outside of City Hall.

After taking 15 minutes to settle the intern down and send her home – she was the daughter of one of the community's leading attorneys – he started for the publisher's office in a near rage.

"You're gonna want me to shut this door," Cratty insisted as he entered the room not bothering to take a seat.

The publisher, with little more than a hint of what was to follow, wanted the door left ajar.

"I'm going to make this short and sweet," Cratty opened, as it was so quiet throughout the rest of the building, you'd have thought the place had suddenly been evacuated.

"If you ever come into my newsroom and put on an erratic display like you did today, I'm gonna rip off that bald head of yours and shit down your neck.

"You may not know this," he continued, "but after the little horror show you just put on in my newsroom, if we

114

caught the woman you're so irrationally obsessed with while she was fucking the local bishop and pilfering the poor box with a free hand, we wouldn't have a leg to stand on. We'd be liable for a charge of slander and everybody in this newsroom would be a witness for the plaintiff. You are really a fucking idiot."

The silence was deafening as Cratty exited. He found out, not too long after that, that there was rumored to be an office pool on just what date Cratty might kill the publisher with his bare hands.

But, other than that particularly unpleasant half of his chores, Cratty enjoyed most of his stay in the Southwest.

His new wife, of course, didn't think that much of the arrangement, with her serving as publisher back in Livingstone and him 1,500 miles west in New Mexico.

He would always joke that he enjoyed being married to a publisher because he could finally do to one of them what he was certain they'd been doing to him for years. Being the kind of woman she was, she always seemed to take it as the jest it was meant to be.

But, like most of his stops in the business, Cratty didn't let his duties of monitoring the madman chained to the wall in the front office stop his professional approach. And, as he soon discovered, the fields of northern New Mexico were full of just as rich a harvest as he'd ever seen.

There might have been a little extra advantage offered by the fact that the town of 20 some thousand was surrounded by the world's largest Indian Reservation.

Reservations provide an interesting look at what more than 200 years of failed national policy had done for the continent's first human inhabitants. It wasn't enough to infect, starve, shoot and literally herded a race of human beings onto some of the most worthless expanse of land on the planet, we also had to leave them to reside in squalid, sub-human conditions of absolute poverty.

The jobless rate on the "Rez," as locals called it, had to be about 50 percent, if not higher. Jobs were almost non-existent, and the living conditions showed it.

Schools and hospital facilities were a disgrace. Thanks to the already short supply of jobs, the education system seemed to provide the only source of steady employment. And Cratty soon learned that the positions were often the result of family and reservation political connections rather than anything remotely resembling competence.

The source of school funding was federal dollars which were doled out on a tribal model of rampant patronage. Cratty soon found school districts spending their federal largesse on lavish seminars in Washington, D.C., and in some cases Hawaiian and other far-off resorts.

When Cratty tried to inform one of the two United States Senators of what he thought was a waste of federal funds that could be better spent on educating Native American kids, the political hack pretended the newspaper editor was speaking another language. He refused to accept the facts and insisted that that could never happen under the current system.

Reservation governance was simply an extension of the practice under which the schools were operated. There was an inner core of power brokers who dished out the jobs, and because there were few if any jobs beyond the graft, everybody seemed to be willing to go along to get along.

It was the most corrupt system Cratty had ever come across, and he'd come across more than his share. People trapped in dire poverty condemned to live on federal handouts funneled through the hands of a bunch of greedy local officials.

The group of middle-schoolers standing in front of him seemed anything but attentive as Cratty guided the 30 or so kids from a reservation school on a tour of his New Mexico publication's press facilities. In fact, they had a collective look more akin to resentment than anything else.

Trying out his rather hard-bitten newsroom sense of humor in an attempt to break the ice, Cratty announced: "Now I have a pretty good idea what the last thing George Custer must have seen at the Little Bighorn."

The youngsters never flinched, but several teachers among them almost rolled on the floor with laughter.

A newspaperman of Cratty's proclivities finds a lot of fertile ground in Indian country. If it's not the white population making money off the natives, it's the Indian politicians feathering their own nests.

Unfortunately, the ground in Indian country was not fertile for much else.

One such local pol was a Navajo who purported to be a "medicine man" and was also an elected member of the local county board. The man would later be accused of sexual harassment and assault, but he initially came across Cratty's radar for grossly overcharging the county for mileage reimbursement.

It wound up that the county attorney, who was serving on an interim basis, demanded that the board member repay a couple a thousand dollars in overages.

After a few months of dragging his feet, the small-time embezzler finally paid up.

On another occasion, a tribal police car pulled over Cratty's wacky publisher on an interstate highway running through the western New Mexican desert. In the confrontation that followed, the Indian cop pulled a pistol and demanded the publisher exit his vehicle.

Cratty had no doubt that his boss probably aggravated the situation and deserved a good deal of the blame, but he also knew that the last thing an American Indian tribe in prime tourist country needed was the chance that visitors would be subject to random stops by reservation cops on a clearly marked national thoroughfare.

For only being in the area less than 11 months, Cratty didn't find it too hard to stir quite a bit of shit, as he was wont to do.

On any American reservation, the selling and consumption of alcohol is strictly prohibited, which turns out to be an open invitation for somebody, usually white, to make a buck. Alcoholism is a raging problem on the Rez, leading to what is an open wound in Native American society.

It's the first time Cratty came across the practice of drug stores having to place their stocks of hair spray under lock and key, limiting the amount purchased and to the people making the purchase.

The reason for the proscription was the thousands of Indians who buy and strain the alcohol content from the spray cans, mixing the resulting liquid with Kool-Aid or other soft drinks for the purpose of inebriation.

Cratty was once directed to what he thought was a common trash dump within yards of a reservation drug store filled with thousands of discarded hair spray cans.

He also managed to leave his young staff quite a bit wiser and more able to ply their trade during his New Mexico stint.

During the sexual harassment trial of the county board member, Cratty sent a young woman on her first trial assignment up against a noon deadline. The paper went to press between noon and 12:30 six days a week and the reporter called Cratty at about 11:50 a.m.

"They just broke for lunch," she reported, then asked if she should stay through the break and put a story together for the next day's edition.

"You can stay through the break and cover the afternoon session, but first we're gonna put together a story for today's edition," Cratty ordered the young woman. She was quite confused and wanted to know what she was to do next.

"Just tell me what happened this morning in court," he began, "and we're going to write this story over the phone!"

Once she got the fact that Cratty was dead serious, she did just fine.

It was a trick he'd learned during his initial try at investigative reporting during his racetrack collaborations

Cratty had always been a big believer in the "beat" system, where a reporter is given a certain area of responsibility, such as education, city government or cops to cover. Regularly plied beats with live sources were the best way to gather news no matter where that news was coming from.

Most all the staff had no problem with the concept, but Cratty soon found he had to make at least one big adjustment.

One of his female reporters, who was not without talent, was obviously using her beat to pad her expenses. She'd log at least one round-trip per week of 100-plus miles for what she said was a meeting with a confidential source.

Now, Cratty already had a two-man bureau in that small Burg and never received anything remotely based on any such source.

His response was to have the woman switched to another beat, which she promptly refused, and she went over Cratty's head to the wacko publisher and his dad. The old man set up a meeting to clear the air.

Just prior to the closed-door session, Cratty was told by the idiot publisher, who had the morals of a motherfucking rattlesnake, that this particular reporter is a "good piece of ass" and he shouldn't take everything so seriously.

Cratty heard the old man and the reporter out and then informed them that she will either accept the new beat or exit the building.

She decided to give up the ghost and accept the change, not wishing to get off the gravy train just yet.

In all the jumping around in Cratty's career, he never got the job he really wanted.

Growing up he'd always been impressed with the sports pages of a newspaper, The Pecatonica Star. And when he found himself covering sports professionally early in his career, he was still in awe of that publication.

He came within a breath of landing a position at the Pecatonica paper while he was making quite a name for himself as a local investigative reporter during the early to mid-1970s.

However, fate intervened, and it might have coincided with the investigative work he was doing at the track.

His first wife had expressed some interest in indulging in her first taste of marijuana. It seemed all the rage at the time and a co-worker offered a small sample to avoid having to procure the stuff on the street.

He brought it home and Cat stashed it in a kitchen cabinet and completely forgot about it. She certainly never tried it, but that forgotten bit of drugs would come back to haunt him.

While he and his partner were engaged in the track flap, there was also a probe into a local sportsbook, the county sheriff's office would serve an early morning warrant at the Cratty residence where they simply walked over to the kitchen cabinet and confiscated the small amount of weed.

During the same span of time, Cratty and his wife were completing the adoption process of a new born. They'd discovered that they wouldn't be able to have another child, so they set their sights on a little girl.

Nobody seemed to know just how the local County Mounty's knew exactly where to look or even why they targeted the Cratty home.

It had crossed his mind that the track probe and the perfectly veiled threat he'd received earlier, as a result, had a hand in the whole mess. But, despite the fact the encounter kept playing in his head for years after the fact, Cratty never felt like pursuing the issue beyond that point.

Not wanting to complicate the adoption, Cratty just took the brunt of the legal hassle.

Now, owing to the relentless editorial pressure on local law enforcement for its inability to ferret out rampant sports betting in the county seemingly going on right under their noses, the local district attorney turned the tables on Cratty's executive editor. In front of a grand jury, specifically called to examine the newspaper probe, the editor was blind-sided with questions about the Cratty drug raid.

The result was six months of probation for the sports writer/investigative reporter and the loss of his byline for roughly two of those months.

There were any number of theories in the newsroom as to just how the whole thing went down and its convenient timing.

The possible job at the only paper he ever really wanted to work at had suddenly dried up and Cratty was left with a bad taste in his mouth, only the first as it would turn out in regard to newspapering.

About six months later, Cratty would leave the publication for a job in public relations at the same local racetrack under new ownership he'd pried into for the previous 18 months.

And, he remembered telling himself at the time that he would never go back to a newsroom.

But, as is so often the case, the best laid plans of mice, men and newspaper hacks often go astray.

The best thing about the dust up, his wife and he were the proud parents of a beautiful baby girl, who, along with her older sister, would end up being the rock of that newspaper hacks life.

8. Nothing to Write Home About

"P.J.! Come on in," said Welsh as he stepped from his office with a smile and handed the guy manning the reception desk a brown file with one hand and ushered Cratty into his office with the other.

Cratty made the 100-mile round trip twice a month to the Viet Nam Vets Center in northwest Illinois near the home he and Beth shared. He had started the counseling sessions a couple of years after coming back from his stint in Texas in the early 1990s, when the anger just seemed to well up inside of him to the point where he felt like the top of his head was coming off for the pain.

He'd find himself in a rage over something he was watching on TV at one moment and then be choking back tears to the point of pain at the next.

And it really seemed like he and Welsh, who was a Marine in 'Nam himself, had established something of a rapport. In fact, Welsh was probably the first Marine that Cratty had ever said more than two civil words to, ever.

Paratroopers and Marines do not mix well, as Cratty would tell just about anyone.

"I had that dream again," said Cratty as he finally situated himself, slouching in a reasonably comfortable low-backed chair.

"The one with the old man?" asked Welsh, having heard the story at least twice a month since the two started these little bullshit sessions some year-and-a-half earlier. The counselling started after Cratty had moved back to Illinois and stopped at two other newspapers following eight years in Texas.

"Yeah. It's one of those things that're never far from the surface."

Two squads had been on a stint out in the boonies, looking for "Charlie." Whenever they found him, they'd either mark the spot on a map, call in an artillery strike or, if it was within range, an airstrike if they could find birds in the area.

They were on their way back to base, which at the time was a spot just west of Tuy Hoa – a small town below a ridge on the South China Sea along Highway 1 about halfway between Nha Trang and Qui Nhon.

Somebody, the best he could remember toward the front of the line, spotted some young girls working in a field with what looked like their grandfather.

Cratty couldn't recall just who came up with the plan and even if it was all that clearly articulated, but one or two guys decided to take one of the girls, none of whom looked more than 13 or 14 years old, into the bushes.

Nobody, Cratty included, said a word; they simply stood by and let it happen. Even though they were all fully aware of what was going on, no one had the moral fortitude or nerve to speak up.

"You blame yourself," said Welsh.

"And, why shouldn't I? Believe me, if I could somehow find a way to lift this goddamned thing off my shoulders, I'd have done it by now.

"I've carried this around for almost 30 years now, and there's absolutely no excuse I can satisfy myself with," he ran on. "And I've got two daughters myself; how in the hell can I ever explain this to them?"

"You've always blamed yourself," continued the Marine, "and from the looks of things, you'll carry that with you forever.

"Now, the question seems to me, 'Can you live with that?' Because, right now that seems to be the most important thing from your point of view."

It was always there, just under the surface, and Cratty couldn't really remember a day during those close to three decades that he hadn't lived with it.

"I have absolutely no idea," Cratty said in a response that was always more reflex than reason.

Since the birth of his own daughters several years before, the burden had grown exponentially. Here he was, the father of two little girls – or at least they used to be little – and he kept playing this incident over and over in his head almost every day since Tuy Hoa.

And that sense of shame would only grow when he became the grandfather of two beautiful little girls, years later.

That old man standing in the burning hot sun that day, probably not a lot older than Cratty was then, could just as easily have been him under different circumstances, and the boiling confusion inside of him just wouldn't stop.

These meetings were anything but standard psychobabble, "let the loony run on for the 50-minute hour." The two Viet Nam veterans really seemed to connect.

"But I can't get over the fact I never said anything, to anybody!" Cratty would always respond. "And not once since that day…you're the only one I've ever talked about it with. I could never hope to explain it to my wives.

"They'd have looked at me like I was some kind of monster," he went on. "And just what could I say to try and explain myself?"

"Have you ever thought that you've been dealing with it in your own unique way? That that's the reason you do what you do?" Welsh asked, striking an almost instant chord.

Suddenly, the rush he always felt when one of his more explosive pieces came together and appeared in print made perfect sense. It was as close to an epiphany as Cratty would ever be, but it had no effect on how he felt about the incident or himself.

"You mean, like always being so goddamned hot to find the dirt and spilling it for everyone to see?"

"Exactly! Seems to me that's why you're so fuckin' driven in what you do in the newspaper business," Welsh replied

"But that's not enough to make up for all this shit running around in my head," Cratty offered. "I still stood there, said nothing, and let it happen."

"So, you sound like you suddenly want to excuse yourself and all this will go away. It will never excuse the thing and your part in it, and it's never going to go away," countered Welsh. "What you have to do is learn to live with it."

Yes, that was true, because it was never going to go away and there was nothing even remotely resembling absolution in his future.

18 and 19-year-old kids shouldn't be put into situations of life and death with loaded weapons and a poorly formed moral compass. But our species continues to put them there and then wonder why we have such fucked-up outcomes.

Makes you wonder why so many are still so surprised when all those kids come back to the real world so screwed up, as Welsh was always quick to explain anytime he and Cratty got together.

No, Pat E. Cratty's oldest son was no longer a patriot. That was something else the old man had been right about.

Actually, Cratty knew more than he was telling about that white-hot day southwest of Tuy Hoa.

First, he was profoundly ashamed, and he certainly couldn't conjure up anything remotely like hatred for anybody else in this recurring nightmare of his. They were all in a brotherhood, a camaraderie that was closer than marriage, family, or anything else on this earth.

So, while he was all too ready to spill the beans on all misdeeds and miscreants in his professional life, he couldn't spare the same effort for retribution for himself and all those inhabiting this horrific slideshow that rattled around in his mind.

To tell the truth, Cratty could never remember who took part in the proceedings that day. No names attached to the murky faces ever came with the dreams and perhaps, deep down inside, Cratty was just as certain that all of those on that day, including himself, were as equally at fault as the rapists.

But it made no difference, there was no explanation that satisfied his conscience or sense of justice. And he knew it never would. If there was a God, and he wasn't quite sure anymore, he was sure he hadn't heard the last of that moment.

If someone tries to tell you that war doesn't change people, he is either completely full of shit or simply trying to put a brave face on a desk job he fell into in Saigon.

It takes, according to Army statistics, seven people in the rear to keep one combat soldier in the line. That would indicate that the overwhelming majority of those who served in 'Nam were anything but your typical grunts. And Cratty was just as certain that anybody who talked with any pride about their stay "over the pond" was certainly a member of that overwhelming majority.

But no matter what particular slot a guy might have filled in 'Nam, one thing was certain, everybody who spent time "in the land of the sliding doors and slant eyed whores" was profoundly changed by the experience.

It took Cratty just hours to discover the depth of that metamorphosis.

He and a guy named Standard, a leg from the 1st Division he'd met on the flight back from Saigon, staggered into a fancy restaurant high on a hill in San Francisco in late June 1966. They were looking to kill a little time between touching down outside the Bay Area at Edwards Air Force Base and going out to the Frisco airport to catch different flights back to their respective hometowns.

"Hey, man, I'm going for a leak," Standard said just after they'd placed an order for steaks "burnt to a crisp and smothered in Heinz 57 and French Fries with real catsup."

"Sir, I'm afraid I'm going to have to ask you to leave," Cratty heard the maître d say over his shoulder.

At first, he wasn't really sure the voice was talking to him between being drunk and all the noise in the background. As he turned, the guy all decked out in a tux pointed to Standard, who'd decided to take his piss in the white marble fountain which graced the center of the dining room.

"So, what's the problem?" was the last thing Cratty, who couldn't for the life of him figure what was out of place in the scene, said as a couple of busboys helped the inebriated duo to the street.

Neither of the two drunks was about to put up a fuss over the incident, as they were both under the legal drinking age, which was another sign of the times. A world full of kids who were old enough to fight, die, surrender arms, legs and sanity, but not to drink or vote for the people who'd sent them off.

If he hadn't quite got the message in Frisco, Cratty was made painfully aware of just how much he had changed since the boat trip to 'Nam a couple of days later back home.

The difference between less than civilized conditions he'd been used to overseas and the "real world" became embarrassingly clear as he sat down with his family – Mom, Dad, Sister, Brother, and Grandma Harriett – for their first real evening meal since Cratty had arrived back from the war.

He'd ordered a thick steak, French fried potatoes, and real catsup. After returning from 'Nam, the need for real catsup took on an oversized role for many G.I.s.

The Vietnamese were clueless about the eating habits of Americans and what passed for catsup in Southeast Asia was crushed, peeled tomatoes floating in water in an old Heinz bottle.

Looking across the family's long kitchen table during his first meal back, Cratty spied the mashed potatoes in a bowl at the far end and blurted the abrupt command: "Pass the fucking potatoes."

The look on the face of his devout Irish-Catholic grandmother's face was like she'd just come by mistake in the presence of the devil on judgement day. She was of a long-gone generation who actually believed in the personification of evil.

You could hear the tires of cars passing on the street outside for the stone-cold silence. The only one in the room besides Cratty who seemed unaffected by the verbal misstep was his dad, who had spent time overseas during World War II, was fighting an urge to fall out of his chair and roll on the floor with laughter.

It took a full minute for Cratty to finally realize what he'd just said. And all he could do was look up red-faced and immediately fall all over himself apologizing.

As he was still mulling over the session with Welsh and they're somewhat of a breakthrough, Cratty remembered Sgt. Davis. He was sure Davis was the man most responsible for Cratty still being above ground. He'd always been certain that if Davis had been along that fateful day near Tuy Hoa, he'd have never had to spend the rest of his life blaming himself for something he would never be able to face openly or explain.

He could have been in any other platoon in any other outfit in the United States Army, and he was convinced that without Davis, he wouldn't have survived 'Nam.

The man was the father he couldn't stand before joining the Army and the one man he would look up to for the rest of his life.

Cratty would also remember and often tell the funniest story he'd ever remember from his tour in 'Nam and the platoon sergeant he so admired.

There was this monkey, the kind that every G.I. in country would remember and the day Davis was trying to fit a .50 cal. machine gun to one of the outfits jeeps, which usually mounted a standard M-60 (7.62 NATO variety).

Davis was standing behind the over-sized weapon and one of the ubiquitous jungle monkeys that hung around encampments, leaped onto Sarge's shoulder, and proceeded to try and diddle him in the ear. Davis smacks the animal off his shoulder and it jumps off the jeep's hood and into mid-air attempting to make its escape.

Just then, Davis opens up with the 50 and hits the monkey mid-flight, instantly causing the creature to disintegrate.

That story would be told and retold a thousand times and was always the favorite of Sarge's grandchildren and just about anybody else who'd stop to listen.

About six months after returning from 'Nam and another six months from his own discharge, Cratty got orders to come to battalion headquarters (1/505th, 82nd Airborne).

When he got there, the first sergeant called him into his office and informed him that he was going to take part in an award ceremony in an hour, where the battalion commander was going to pin a medal on his chest.

"Top, what's this all about?" he asked, shocked by the announcement.

"Seems that you were involved in some night patrol following a rather nasty fire-fight near Tuy Hoa in the Republic of Viet Nam on March 13-14, 1966," the First Shirt rattled off the citation.

"But Top, I don't know what in the hell they're talking about," Cratty was near begging.

And then, when he looked at the paperwork, he thought he'd found an escape clause.

"Top, this award is for Patrick John, my name is Jacob, by this time grasping at straws. There has to be a mistake, and it says here I volunteered. I'll be damned if I ever volunteered for a goddamn thing."

"Son, the United States Army doesn't make mistakes, especially where E/4s such as yourself are concerned," he noted in his usual full-bodied direct order tone.

"Is the serial number correct?" asked the battalion's top NCO.

"Yes, but I really don't know what they're talking about, Top."

"Cratty, you're elected. In just under an hour you're gonna be standing at attention in front of the lieutenant colonel who commands this outfit. He's gonna pin a medal on your chest and you're gonna salute, shake his hand and say, 'Thank you, Sir!'"

Forty-five minutes later, Cratty flashed a crisp salute, shook hands with his commanding officer and sounded an even snappier, "Thank you, sir" without a single hesitation.

Still half asleep on a night when he'd finally found a spot out of the Monsoon rains to catch a quick nap, Cratty was being shaken awake by Sgt. Davis who had just "voluntold" him for a night patrol.

It seemed a line company had tangled with the Viet Cong on a hillside a couple of hundred yards from the Song Ba. The outcome was at least five badly shot-up paratroopers who were in need of a Dustoff chopper medevac which couldn't reach the wounded due to heavy jungle cover and lack of a flat spot to land.

That left it up to the Hawk Platoon (recon) to hump about two miles across the river and through a mine field of unknown origin and depth to retrieve the casualties and take them to a spot more conducive to helicopter extraction.

Unlike the heroic details in the Department of Defense citation, there was certainly no volunteering or bravery involved. In fact, there wasn't a shot fired and the French laid mines were probably much too old to threaten friend or foe.

It really worked out for the best. Cratty never could fall asleep in a driving rainstorm, especially when there were little to no dry spots available.

He'd arrived at Delaware – his last career stop – just six days into the new millennium. It would finally be the place that convinced him that the business was no longer for him.

The business had gone through a complete change in the previous 20 to 25 years, and it had happened without him really noticing at the time. Oh, he knew things were getting steadily different month by month and year by year, but to his way of thinking, it snuck up on him in his sleep.

He guessed that's what everybody told themselves when they reached this stage of their professional lives, but it was true, and these last few years would probably bring him face to face with the reality that he'd outlived his relevance and his chosen profession was in the process of committing an excruciating act of Hari Kari.

"You know," blurted out the Delaware Daily Call photo editor during one of those regular four o'clock budget meetings, where the editors get together around a conference table and discuss the next day's stories, "every time we run one of these priest sex abuse stories, it just gives that victims' group (Survivors Network of those Abused by Priests) a lot of free publicity."

The photo editor was one of those fawning sycophants you find in any work environment and had a Napoleonic complex the size of Texas and probably a dick more conducive to bug-fucking. But there was always his personality that grated on and/or belittled everyone he ever encountered.

Of course, the topic at the heart of this bullshit session in a community that was anywhere from 80 to 90 percent Roman Catholic was of some interest. Delaware was the seat of the state's first Catholic archdiocese, which went back to the French and Spanish settlement of the region.

A former parishioner had filed a multimillion-dollar lawsuit against a former priest in the archdiocese which covered all of the northeast part of the state. It wasn't the first such action against the archdiocese or the priest, who had long since died.

It wasn't so much the eagerness of the photo editor that bothered Cratty, who was in the meeting presenting AP wire offerings for the next day's paper. It was the fact that everybody – from the executive, city, and assistant city editor – seated around the table considering this decision was Catholic. Hell, Cratty himself had been raised in the faith.

In a town that tied to the faith, bad press directed at the local representative of the holy see was a ticklish subject to begin with, but tie that fact to the religious affiliation of the majority of those making such a decision and you've got the makings of a gigantic objectivity problem.

Cratty had only been at the paper a matter of a year or two, and his presence at the meeting was simply a courtesy for the copy desk editor who cleared that day's wire summary.

The conversation didn't last all that long but the outcome was a foregone conclusion: The lawsuit would be bumped from the front page to the inside local.

As it would turn out, a few years later, the archdiocese would agree to a $5-million settlement, which even following the court verdict would be soft peddled in the Daily Call.

That would have been bad enough, but in the Daily Call's haste to kiss the bishop's ring, long before the court ruling, the paper wrote at least one glowing editorial, praising the local church for its handling of the priest molestation scandal that swept through the American Catholic community in the early years of the new millennium. In fact, one editorial was so ridiculously infatuated with the archdiocese that it posited the thought that "if the rest of the nation's dioceses had handled the problem the way Delaware did, there wouldn't be a scandal."

Yeah, right.

That seemed to be the trend as the century changed in much of the newspaper industry, as most local papers found it easier and much less stormy to simply go along with the powers that be. It also reduced the need for extra reporters, as much of the news that was left to print came in the form of news releases and/or "official" phone calls from the very entities that reporters were supposed to be keeping an eye on.

Instead of being the adversarial relationship that once governed the nation's free press, it was now a matter of reading faxed reports from police, city, county, and state offices. Cratty had never heard of such a thing as a "police department spokesman" much before about 1995. And now it seemed that every entity from dogcatcher to hospital and city government had a "spokesman" or more likely in the age of so-called gender equity what they liked to refer to as a "spokesperson."

"I never learned anything from a police spokesman that I couldn't get a better picture of from a face-to-face session with an inside source," explained Cratty to a young police beat reporter late in his career.

"Because, police departments are like any other organization, be it family or corporation," he'd often spout, "There are those who are 'in' and those who are 'out.' Anytime you want to know what's really going on, simply find somebody in each group to tell you their side of the story, and you can pretty much piece the whole thing together in half the time.

"Official spokesmen only give you that part of the story the people who sign their paychecks want you to know. In fact, I've never come across one of 'em who knew his butt from page six!"

But it was always like talking to a wall when he'd espouse his views on the subject to superiors, who were usually half his age and probably weren't even a gleam in their father's eye by the time Cratty had earned his first byline.

First, the concept of beat reporters was ancient history as newsrooms kept cutting staff. That made dependence on news releases even more effective for news sources and the short-staffed media, both print and broadcast.

Then late in the 2000-decade, self-styled newsgroups started popping up, especially of the staunchly conservative persuasion, offering local papers already suffering under staffing shortages free gratis statehouse coverage. It soon became clear what the slant and purpose of said stories being offered was.

Groups fronting for the Koch Brothers and like interests were pushing a particular political point of view and money and resource starved local outlets were co-opted into passing off propaganda as real news.

But the unbelievable thing was, the latest generation of journalists wasn't the least bit interested in what those with decades of experience had to say. The last 15 years or so of his career, Cratty was never once asked his opinion by one of those youngish, middle management types half his age.

This younger crop of scribe was also remarkably deficient in the one trait Cratty was convinced every reporter worth his notepad had to be imbued with cynicism and a strong distrust of all official pronouncements.

They seemed to arrive fresh out of journalism school these days with the infantile belief that "NO ONE EVER LIES!"

Now, that's a far cry from back in the day when the rule was that absolutely everyone lies, especially when it reflects on their reputation both professionally and personally.

"I never met a single human being who was either willing or capable of telling me something bad about themselves," said Cratty so many times over the years that he'd lost count. "They save that kind of shit for confession or their shrinks.

"I was skeptical of every official pronouncement I ever heard. And I can count the number of times such officials were actually telling the truth on one hand. And I've talked to thousands of such individuals."

He was also never shy about his less than glowing opinion of both TV and radio news teams.

"It takes what, five minutes to get enough material for a 30-second clip on the nightly news?" he was fond of asking.

"If you can tell a story in 30 seconds, it's neither a story nor worth telling."

9. A Nine-Fingered Paratrooper

A member of an early Long-Range Recon lost the ring finger and his wedding ring during a hairy extraction not long after the recon platoon started perfecting the practice of such excursions. It was a lesson that proved experience is the best teacher, despite what the younger generation in any endeavor might think.

The patrol was out for about five days, in the low rolling hills in the western Song Ba river valley, about 15 to 20 miles southwest of the coast.

The area was crawling with Victor Charlies and their North Vietnamese cousins.

That six-man patrol must have driven 'em nuts, calling in airstrikes and artillery at all hours.

Anyway, the welcome was beginning to wear just a bit thin toward the end of the first week. It must have been that the local VC commander was getting just a little tired of dodging the high explosives and napalm.

"Look at that silly fucker," laughed DeBonis as he yanked at Cratty's fatigue jacket.

There's something that war does to your sense of humor, as well.

This crazy fucker was running around like a chicken with his head cut off while incoming 155 howitzer shells were falling like raindrops. Just as Cratty looked up, it appeared almost as if a round fell right at the dumbass' feet, like he was catching it in his outstretched arms.

It goes off and there wasn't enough left of the poor bastard to put in a tin can.

Charlie had to know that there was someone watching him. You don't suddenly find yourself on the receiving end of all that ordinance and believe it's a coincidence.

Things were getting a little too hot for the recon patrol.

So, Sgt. Davis called the squad together on the fifth evening and took a vote, not a usual tact for the hard-bitten airborne ranger non-com, but under the circumstances, it seemed appropriate.

"We're in some deep shit here," he opened. "We gotta decide on trying to walk out of Indian Country, hoping we can avoid contact with the very edgy hostile Indians, or try and line up an early extract."

"We haven't got a fuckin' chance of humping our way outta here, Sarge," added one of us. "These gooks are as thick as flies on a pile of shit in this valley."

So, the squad voted for an extraction, four days ahead of schedule and most likely 10 to 15 miles from the spot it was originally set for.

The cavalry was contacted, and it could make it at about sunrise the next day.

Just had to sit and wait for eight and a half hours. As Cratty recalled, the night before the extraction was spent by stretching ponchos between the branches of some bushes on a rise above the agreed upon pickup spot. The practice was the best way to get a little extra water, as the team was still some distance from any aqua, and nobody seemed anxious to take a walk to find out just where it was.

It was a trick that had worked previously and was helped by the fact that the humidity in 'Nam was always about the same as the temperature, between 90 to 99 percent.

When the Hueys came swooping down into the lush green valley from the east, the squad started for the rendezvous.

They didn't want to get there too early and attract any unwanted attention.

The agreed upon procedure was for the choppers to make at least two faints before dropping in for the pickup.

But this bird must have had a cherry on the stick. The Huey made one pass down the north side of the valley, swung back south across the river and then made a beeline for the patrol's position just south of the Song Ba.

No faint, not even a hint. He swung in and the patrol had no choice, they had to pile in or turn and walk out.

Of course, the presence of a flight of choppers making passes on hilltops was a dead giveaway. There was really only one option, and there it was swooping in just over the ground 50 feet ahead.

The entire squad made a mad dash from all directions, diving in.

But this time, the LZ was starting out red-hot.

Another patrol of VC, most likely already looking for the GIs after the previous week's work, opened up from across the river.

As they dove in from both sides, everybody grabbing onto anything they could get, we could hear the rounds whizzing through the wide-open chopper doors and pinging off the skids.

It must have been about that time that a member of the group raised his hand, probably looking for something else to grab hold of.

"Shit!" he cried out. "Goddamn, I'm hit."

"How bad is it!" yelled Davis.

"Motherfucker, those sons of bitches shot my fuckin' finger off…and it's my goddamned ring finger. My fuckin' wedding ring's gone."

Later Davis would be told there were upwards of 100 holes in that chopper.

The next time the same situation presented itself, and as luck would have it, they knew it would, Davis looked up and in a clear, major, military tone barked, "Fuck it, I'm walkin'!"

10. S'ter Harbor Police

It didn't take long for Cratty to discover that he'd soon get crossways in Delaware, just like he'd done at a dozen other stops on the map.

He didn't get back into the column harness right off, having signed on to the copy desk and trying to keep a low profile at the first job he had that showed some sort of post-career security.

It was an ESOP, locally owned communications chain with a 401(k) and what for him was the best wages he'd ever scored at any newspaper.

But he should have known that wouldn't last. Just like all the other jobs he'd had in the business, Cratty had to be the center of attention. And, as it turned out, it would be a ride that would finally get him to kick the entire profession cold turkey.

It took a year or more after arriving – within days of the new millennium – before Cratty was granted a column in Delaware, where he was featured two days a month on the opinion page. Since he'd churned out up to three columns per week at some papers, the offer at first seemed a little beneath his station.

The nitpicking suggestions by the editorial page editor, who was also the publication's executive editor, seemed a little annoying at first. That would also change, but he humored the management just enough in an attempt at finally getting along.

Cratty was not one of those you could say "played well with others." In fact, he seemed to be at his best when he alone stood at the barricade and had the rest of the world for a target. He thought it made it so much easier to tell the good guys from the bad.

Still stinging from the paper's stance in regards of the Catholic Church child abuse flare-up, Cratty decided to dredge up some of his combat scars earned in 10 years of parochial school education under the "penguins" – nuns, as he and most everyone else who went to a parochial school called them. Now, this would have been bad enough in such a predominantly Catholic community, but it was doubly explosive in a county where no less than three different Catholic women's religious orders were headquartered.

He recalled his battles with one S'ter Harbor Police back in eighth grade.

He informed the reading audience of the fact that Harbor Police was the mother of night baseball in America. She won this distinction due to her penchant for always rooting out her male students' habit of trying to listen to each fall's World Series during school hours.

Back in the day, the Series was only contested during daylight hours, which naturally conflicted with the time of day younger fans were in class.

Some of Cratty's classmates had some ingenious methods of trying to get around her crusade. Fake arm casts implanted with transistor radios were perhaps the most common. But nothing seemed foolproof.

It was awfully hard to put one over on Ole Harbor Police, perhaps the fact that all these fake casts and other paraphernalia always seemed to crop up the same time each year was a dead giveaway.

One day, during the 1960 classic between the Pittsburgh Pirates and New York Yankees, a particularly painful year for the national pastime, Harbor Police caught one of Cratty's friends trying to listen to the cataclysmic seventh game through a device hidden in a neck/head bandage.

OK, so it wasn't the smartest move. But, what can you expect of boys at the dawn of the 1960s? The cultural revolution was still a few years off, after all.

She was probably years ahead of her time, Ole S'ter Harbor Police. Actually, she was a bit younger than most of the nuns and in fact, she, aka Barbara Therese, should probably be credited with having a hand in the invention of "stealth technology" as well as night baseball.

Back in the day, most nuns would always sound an early warning as kids heard their beads rattling as they floated – funny you never seemed to see their feet hit the floor – down the hallways. Not S'ter Harbor Police, she'd simply pick up the beads and unleash an unannounced flanking movement.

Of course, the columns devoted to the exaggerated religious antagonist weren't well received in several circles in Delaware, where invariably one or two letters with the return address of one of the local orders, would contend that Cratty was exaggerating and/or outright fabricating his recollections.

Admittedly, Cratty was not above embellishing his tales.

But those adversaries found it a lot harder to erase the memories of the thousands of other Catholics among the readership who suffered under pretty much the same oppression.

Then there was the time Cratty recalled being slapped in the hallway by Harbor Police after an incident involving water balloons tossed from the second-floor fire escape onto the girls' playground. In those days, the boys and girls weren't allowed to mix during recess – or anyplace else, for that matter.

"Who's responsible for that stunt?" asked Harbor Police as she sashayed into the classroom. Of course, Cratty, who was never shy when it came to taking credit for his handiwork, stood up immediately.

"Well, that's not a surprise! I knew that coming down the hall. So, who else was in on this?" As was usually the case, no one else had the guts to join in the confession, too afraid of the consequences, which were usually swift and corporal.

Harbor Police had a special row in her classroom known as "Sleepy Hollow," where she decided to segregate her problems from the rest of the class. Of course, Cratty and one other kid were the only two to spend the entire year in Sleepy Hollow, where Cratty was designated as mayor.

The only saving grace for Cratty, as it would be for the rest of his life, was the fact that his sense of humor never let him take anything seriously enough to bother him. But unfortunately, the same couldn't be said for the other permanent resident of Sleepy Hollow, who didn't fare quite so well following the completion of his sentence and readmittance to regular society.

Once, the school's principal – a pigmy of a nun – called Cratty and a co-conspirator into her inner sanctum for some misdeed or other and had to literally leap off her feet to slap his much taller partner in crime. Cratty cracked up laughing, and she turned with the look of vengeance on her face, asking if "Mr. Cratty" thought it was funny enough to want to share in the reckoning.

"I don't care if you hit me with a brick, S'ter, that was one of the funniest things I've ever seen!"

The diminutive woman had to turn away so that the two penitents wouldn't see her fighting back the urge to laugh herself.

He couldn't tell you just when his chosen profession had changed, but during the last 20 some years of it, he was aware that something just didn't seem right.

He got a large dose of the malady at Delaware when a publisher informed the newsroom staff that in the interest of "complete objectivity," reporters and editors were not allowed to take part in the quadrennial Iowa presidential caucuses.

It's a peculiarly Hawkeye practice that occurs as the first battle of the nation's presidential primary season. Those who take part must show up on a usually bitterly cold Iowa winter night and display their preference by gathering in groups supporting particular candidates.

The event is practiced differently depending on the two parties involved. Democrats actually have to get up and gather together, showing their preference, while Republicans use a secret ballot. Meanwhile, caucusgoers are required to sit through up to three hours at these sessions, while a final tally is arrived at.

However, no distinction between the party affiliations was made in the newsroom edict. This pompous order from on high pissed Cratty off, and when he heard the excuse, he reached boiling point.

"We're trying to present this news organization as completely nonpartisan," was the reason given.

Cratty openly expressed his wonder at just what the reading public probably thought of the fact that several managerial types of this "objective" organization, just a floor below the newsroom, showed their political preferences openly with thousand-dollar donations given with full disclosure on campaign reports published in the same newspaper.

And all this in the same publication that, due to the religious bias of editors, buried a story on an eventually successful multimillion-dollar suit filed against the Delaware Archdiocese during the height of the priest abuse scandal.

If he learned nothing else from these encounters and others over the years, Cratty learned that in this business, hypocrisy knew no bounds.

The "no newsroom participation in caucuses" edict came down as the nation looked toward the 2008 presidential primary season, and Cratty wasn't quite sure if the fact that a black man running in that particular race might not have something to do with the whole kerfuffle. But later, it seemed to have everything to do with it.

On Election Night 2008, the newsroom staff gathered as it always did on such occasions and was informed, for the first time ever, that emotional displays of any kind regarding the night's outcome would be frowned upon by the management.

So, perhaps the most moving election results in American history were to be greeted by professional stoicism and minus so much as a whimper.

It was the most emotional election night of Cratty's almost 40 plus years in the business and it was all he could do – child of the 1960s that he was – to not break down in tears.

But, as today's newsroom managers would insist, grown journalists don't cry.

And he would also learn something else in his time at Delaware: In this business, you couldn't ever go home.

It might have been the same if he'd had the chance to go back home as a yeoman scribe. There were too many family members, friends, and the knowledge of just where all the bodies were buried to give you a disinterested or objective view of the landscape.

And certainly, it would be next to impossible to practice the kind of journalism that Cratty was so good at amongst friends and family. So, as he passed his fourth decade in journalism, he was thankful that he was never put to the test on that count.

But he came across more than his share of those who were put to such a test, and he never once remembered anyone who'd passed it. Mostly, it was those who were born and raised in a community where they practiced the profession who lacked the nerve to go unaffected by such hometown bias.

The business, much to Cratty's consternation, was not only playing soft toss with those holding political office, legal responsibility and/or economic position but had a distinct penchant for piling on those lacking the same.

Cratty noticed this first at Delaware during the 2004 presidential primaries. Former U.S. Sen. Carol Moseley Braun (D-Ill) competed in the early going of the Iowa Democratic Caucuses but withdrew before caucus night.

Upon her withdrawal, Delaware's Daily Call, whose newsroom was led by individuals who either were born and raised in the community or had spent decades there, took a backhanded swipe at the candidate as she exited. The message essentially amounted to: "Who did she think she was fooling by contending for her party's nomination?" There was no purpose for the editorial comment, other than the fact the author was sure Braun, an African American woman, lacked any support among white eastern Iowa readers.

However, the worst was yet to come.

"Well certainly, the fact the guy committed suicide showed his guilt."

Cratty was stunned when he heard those words tumble from the mouth of a colleague.

A local man had been charged with the murder of his wife, a teacher, in a gruesome case that understandably shocked the community.

The accused's family – which unfortunately happened to be from out of town – had taken a second mortgage on their home to help the suspect both hire an attorney and cover his bail.

During the bond proceedings, the defense had wondered if it might be possible to place the resulting amount in an escrow account to draw interest.

It was not an unusual request, but you'd have thought the suspect was asking for the key to the cell-door by the editorial page response, which was something to the effect of "Well, is there anything else we can do for you, Mr....?"

The next day, the accused was found dead of asphyxiation in the same garage where his wife's body was found.

The same person who penned the sorry excuse for an editorial mocking the accused's court filing also openly opined, "Well certainly, the fact the guy committed suicide showed his guilt."

And, if there was any doubt that the publication's management disapproved of this crudity that was put to rest several days later when the suspect's paid obituary appeared.

Not wanting to leave the slightest hint among its readers just where the paper stood – and disregarding the fact that the dead man had not been convicted in a court of law – the publisher added a positively gut-wrenching editor's note to the family's grieving remembrance of their son.

In that note, the publisher – a paperboy promoted to his level of incompetence – wasted neither compassion nor decency in making sure that readers knew that the words of grief appearing above were those of the man's family and not shared by "this publication."

Yet another example of a bean counter elevated to the position of newsroom executive and a particularly obscene one at that.

"I've written some pretty caustic pieces in my time and several I'm not particularly proud of," Cratty said to his copy desk cohorts later. "But, I have never, in my more than

65 years on this planet, ever read something so profoundly disturbing and vile. And I don't think I've ever written something that might be connected to a suicide, either."

It was certainly the most disgusting thing he'd ever seen in print. But he also remembered a time he once fought another battle in direct opposition to a family's obituary wishes.

He wasn't without journalistic skeletons of his own.

Like the Thanksgiving edition in Warren, when the word "FUCK" appeared dead center in the year's largest printing of the Reporter News. Adding to the embarrassment, the edition was delivered free of charge to every household in the town of some 11,000 residents.

Cratty was then the executive editor of the Reporter News in the mid '90s and had attempted to fill out the offering by allowing his staff to submit their favorite columns from the previous year. Unbeknownst to him, there was a funny little game that was played by staffers before his arrival earlier that year, whereby they would purposely place objectionable words and phrases amid items as a joke on those who edited them.

Then the authors simply stored the pieces unchanged in their computer files.

As it turned out, the joke was on Cratty and the unfortunate author of the column in question. But it was indeed his fault for not reading each and every offering.

That was the first time in his career that Cratty offered his sincere resignation to a publisher, and the first time seeing such a bomb in print almost sent him to his knees, sick to his stomach. The Warren publisher, in possession of just a bit more mercy than was probably due, did not accept Cratty's resignation.

He'd only ever heard of one other such instance, but luckily it was expunged with a chisel and hammer on an old hot lead press roll before reaching the street.

Similar to the Warren prank, reporters at his hometown paper years earlier would write what they thought to be funny obits to tickle the fancy of colleagues. One such obit involved an elderly woman who had died by falling into her outhouse and drowning.

As one might have guessed, the foul-mouthed graveyard humor noted "76 years of Mrs. (So-and-so's) shit caught up with her Thursday." While the press was running, a sharp editor on the desk found the obit on a proof sheet and promptly chiseled the offending lead graph on the fly.

As for obituary offences, Cratty had his own, which probably left him little room to talk, but for a completely different reason.

A middle-aged, special needs man with a love of animals, especially horses, died while Cratty was the executive editor in Livingstone.

The man's free obit came in from the local mortuary, and almost as the item was crossing the front desk, Cratty got a call from a local doctor. Apparently, the man, who spent most of his time working the stables at Chicago-area racetracks, also had a son with a woman he'd met while working in the horse barns.

The child was profoundly handicapped and lived with his mother in Chicago. The reason the doctor knew of the situation was because, besides serving as the gentleman's personal physician, he also used to provide transportation for the guy to see the child. He informed Cratty of the situation and he immediately checked with the funeral home director, who said he would contact the family.

Well, that's when all hell broke loose as a woman speaking for the family, supposedly the man's mother, called Cratty and insisted that the child had no right to be included in the obituary.

And it might have ended there, save for the tact the understandably angry woman took with the editor at that point.

"That kid will never read that obit and he'll never know about all this!" she shouted over the phone.

"You're right, ma'am, that child will probably never know about his father's passing. But, lady, I'll know! And if you want to take this to the next level and file any legal action over the situation, who do you think is gonna look like the biggest asshole in this story?"

The family was later allowed to run its own obituary, sans child.

Yes, journalism had certainly changed since Cratty broke into the business in 1970 at LaMotte, where he really learned almost everything he ever knew about the industry in a whirlwind 18 months.

He learned that the job of newspaper reporters is to gather, compile and write in as a readable form as possible, the truth or as close to that laudable goal as they could. He also learned that there were any number of obstacles placed in the path of such a task and that all of them were individuals and/or situations that wished to keep those truths from surfacing.

Common wisdom will tell you there are always two sides to every story. But, what "they" don't bother to add is there are most likely two or more different interpretations of truth and the self-interested reasons of those concerned for believing it. Cratty would discover, after decades of butting his head against a wall, that there is only one truth, and everything else is simply how it reflected on those involved.

And therein lies the journalist's conundrum. Everybody sees the same thing differently, and motives are like assholes: everybody's got one.

Nobody's gonna step up to the microphone and lay bare their biggest failings and darkest secrets. That's why the road to the truth is all too often a circuitous route, winding in and out and involving lots of deep ruts.

"Listen," said Cratty on the phone to a district attorney friend of his from Illinois, "is it possible for you to track somebody down with a license plate number?"

"Yeah," answered the county official without even bothering to ask why a guy he hadn't talked to in a couple of years was asking. "It can be done, but you won't be able to do it. The only computer with that kind of information is for law enforcement agencies only."

"Well, now we come to the purpose of this call," quipped Cratty. "Could you run such a plate for me?"

"Sure," said the DA, who didn't hesitate to grant the less than legal request. The two went way back to when Cratty was still a struggling reporter in Illinois and the freshly minted official was not too long in his current post in the prosecutor's office.

"You want I should do it while you wait here on the line?" asked his mark, who added a quick, "Hello, by the way."

It's always helpful in this business to make friends in all the right places. You never know when they're gonna come in handy. It's also a good idea to be nice to the right people on the way up; you'll always meet the same ones on the way down, as they often say.

Not more than five minutes passed on the other end while the DA called over to the county sheriff's dispatch center and had a computer check run.

"Well, I can tell you it's a Florida plate," said his friend, "but you knew that before you called. And I can tell you it's registered to a woman in Clearwater."

"You want the name, age, and address, no doubt?" he asked, and then rattled off the information without waiting for an answer.

"What's this all about, anyway?" said the DA, adding, "Never mind, I'm sure that I'd really rather not know."

That's the best part of friends in the right places, they cut the legwork in half and always want to stay as unconnected to the story as they can for any number of very good reasons.

Cratty had only been in Michigan a few months, when he came across a rather pompous assistant county attorney who seemed to have it in for DUI suspects. He'd built a name for himself by throwing the book at those pulled over in various states of inebriation.

Cratty had latched onto this tale while working on a story in the county attorney's office that involved a female clerk in the department who was reportedly living with a paroled sex offender. The clerk had a teenage daughter of her own living in the home, and the ex-husband/father of the teen was putting up quite a legal fuss over the arrangement.

In the course of that story, he'd learned that one of the office's prosecutors so hot to cuff and jail driving under the influence offenders was himself not averse to hoisting a few and then getting behind the wheel.

In fact, a source in the cop shop had informed Cratty that this assistant had been pulled over recently with the result that, instead of being booked, he was chauffeured home by the officer who made the stop and given help retrieving his auto along the busiest street in the tourist town on the southeast shore of Lake Michigan.

The only thing the source had for the story was directions to the dispatch log that would neatly tie a bow on the package with a license plate of a car being pulled over in the early morning hours of the night in question.

The plate was registered to a woman in Florida who, as luck would have it, was the mother of the hypocrite assistant county attorney at the heart of the inquiry.

It was a slam-dunk, and as it turned out, Cratty only needed to get the attorney on the phone and ask him if he was acquainted with the woman in Florida. There wasn't even any need for taking space in his column. The miscreant resigned on the spot.

"Look, I'm about to go to lunch," said a district attorney, more than 20 years earlier when Cratty was still an up and coming sportswriter/investigative reporter.

"Now, you will notice that on my desk, there is a stack of files. Now they may or may not deal with the probe we just talked about.

"I'll be gone for about 90 minutes," he said. It sounded more like a warning than a polite exchange of pleasantries.

That was the day Cratty knew that the professional connection between the two was a lot closer than it might have been normally. The DA certainly didn't have to risk his career to leave a newspaper reporter with complete access to such a file with no other stipulation than not to remove any of it from his office.

Cratty spent the rest of the 90 minutes reading everything he could with specific attention to testimony given behind closed doors. And when he couldn't read fast enough, he started burning up the xerox machine in the outer office.

The two passed with a mere nod as Cratty was leaving the building, and three days later, the roof came off the probe on the front page of the paper.

The right sources can make an investigative reporter look awfully good. Cratty was sure that Woodward and Bernstein would be nothing more than confused with the name of an obscure law firm if not for the right sources at the right time.

"Deep Throat" had as much if not more to do with the Watergate scandal than the two scribes following the money.

"If given the choice between luck and sources," Cratty once joked, "I'll take sources. Of course, a little luck can't hurt."

11. Another Casualty

The Daily Call was never known for its engrossing opinion page. In fact, local columns were little more than vanilla in flavor, rarely venturing beyond the bounds of polite Midwest hospitality and humor. Besides attempts at lite humor, there wasn't much of real interest.

The canned stuff ranged between centrist to all out right-wing fare.

George Will to Cal Thomas pretty much defined the parameters, with Clarence Page providing one of the few moderate voices.

Most of the editorial page space was devoted once each week to the paper's executive editor, who was not exactly a riveting read.

"That man could put you to sleep recounting the crucifixion!" Cratty would opine from time to time. His usual fare dealt with various changes in the paper's comic page lineup.

It was never anything edgy and even less humorous.

Of course, Cratty's addition to the lineup was somewhat of a shock.

"It's the job of a columnist to get people to read the paper," was the veteran newspaperman's first and only rule. "However, in doing so, it never hurts to also entertain/antagonize the readership a bit, to start and stir the conversation."

And Cratty could entertain/antagonize.

Cratty once opined that he didn't care if you had to steal the paper if you wanted to read it badly enough.

At any paper where he could put his fingers to the keys, the opinion page might have been the best read in the publication.

He was the kind of columnist that also provided an added window into the way things were in the various communities where he practiced his art. Well, art might be a stretch, especially among the extensive list of those who were the subjects of those epistles.

Shortly after he arrived and before he started turning out a column, Delaware's storied meatpacking heritage underwent a massive shift with the purchase of the local operation, which employed upwards of 1,100 by a nationally known competitor. Involved in the offer was a promise to retain the workforce and invest more than $10 million in upgrading the plant.

However, unbeknownst to the local Chamber of Commerce, city fathers and Cratty's newest employer, the object of the exercise was actually to simply close down the competition – a very common practice in the industry, as Delaware was about to learn the hard way.

Cratty, as he did everywhere he landed, started cultivating sources, which usually involved making the acquaintance of as many locals as possible. This was helped by the fact that he was a newspaperman. It was almost second nature at every place from New Mexico, Texas,

Illinois, Michigan, and Iowa in close to 40 years in the business.

In Delaware, Cratty had made the acquaintance of a maintenance man at the local meatpacking plant, which boasted a history that stretched back to the mid-19th century.

The maintenance worker, who lived in the same apartment building, informed Cratty that instead of upgrading the facility, the new management was disassembling the factory's machinery right down to the bolts in the floor.

Cratty immediately informed his superiors and was summarily dismissed as a new arrival with no relevant knowledge of the local community.

"Why, the new owners are investing $10 million in the plant. Why would they do that if they were going to close it down?" was the response.

Cratty responded, "Unless you've got some sort of banking source who's seen that $10 million check, I think we're missing a real story here that could end up affecting quite a lot of people in this town."

Well, the plant never reopened, and with the collapse of the meatpacking industry, the town was left looking for a new economic future.

Now, there was a time when any local paper would have been all over such a story. But, as Cratty was noticing, newspapers, most notably the local variety, were beginning to see themselves as essential cogs in the economic well-being of their communities; they started serving more as cheerleaders for business and a lot less as the watchdogs on that sector and that of the populations' governance.

In short, publications throughout the country, especially in those parts of it he'd practiced in, surrendered to the call of being "just another business" and failed to see themselves as an integral part of a democratic society.

If Thomas Jefferson and the rest of the Founding Fathers had seen the "press" as nothing more than a moneymaking scheme for a few ambitious merchants, why was it enshrined in the nation's founding document? If that were the purpose of the news media, then why leave out grocers, hoteliers, restaurateurs and the rest of the retail class?

After Delaware survived the collapse of meatpacking, a nearly catastrophic blow, city fathers and their chamber sycophants embarked on a whole new economic model: tourism, almost ignoring the disaster that precipitated the major change in the economy.

And, with the help of an $80-million plus investment by a state of Iowa tourism body, the town's Mississippi riverfront was to be transformed into a destination filled with a museum, water-park hotel, and convention center built around a land-based casino, the town's second such gambling operation.

In all the hype, the fact that the town's mayor had a sizeable share in the planned hotel and water park seemed to get lost.

When one of the paper's young city reporters stumbled upon the mayor's ownership, it was no big deal. Because the mayor, who just happened to be the owner of a real-estate firm in town, explained that he avoided any possible conflict of interest by refusing to take part in any of the council debate on the matter. However, he managed to remain in the room while the rest of the city council discussed the matter.

And, according to the city attorney, his vote in favor of accepting the state's largesse was also not a conflict of interest.

Now, no one raised an eyebrow to the fact that everyone else in the council chambers during that vote was well aware of the mayor's substantial investment in the multimillion-dollar project. So, there was nothing to see here, "just move along."

All this, according to the mayor, his attorney, and evidently the newspaper – which promptly endorsed his honor for re-election at the same time – was above reproach.

After the Ice Harbor project and its adoption cooled down, the young reporter who first broke the story was persona non-grata at City Hall. She had to endure some awkward encounters during her daily rounds for a month or so.

Later, another reporter – this time the business writer – came across an exclusive story which involved a local casino license holder and a less than legal political campaign contribution during a race for Iowa governor. The multi-thousand-dollar handout, which was a violation of state law, especially for a licensed casino was paid through a third party by the gambling operation's holding company.

The Delaware paper was privy to the information in facts found in court filings and the admission of at least one state official. Seems the casino threw the third-party bagman under the bus and extricated itself from the indictment by paying a hefty amount – not a fine, according to officials – which was then used to fund further investigation of the matter.

As for the "exclusive," the paper's editor allowed the casino to skip by telling the reporter that "we couldn't run the story without a response from the casino's management."

"Don't you want the story to be fair?" he asked the young female scribe. She countered that the casino had more than enough time to respond to the facts of the story. But it was a futile attempt

That was another feature of local journalism in the 1990s and 2000s. Organizations, both of the business and governmental variety, started hiding behind official flaks referred to as spokespersons.

Handy little built-in defense: Just wait out the response until the story goes cold. And sure enough, the story ran statewide in at least two other newspapers, and no one was the wiser in Delaware because the Daily Call simply inserted a brief in a news roundup, essentially recounting a wire report.

No harm, no foul!

Shortly after the Ice Harbor complex got up and running, the head of the state's tourism body that footed the $80 million boost approached the city for a stadium to house his out of state minor league baseball team.

The pitch was that if the city put up $15 million for a ballpark in the Ice Harbor district, he so kindly provided with state funding, he would in turn, bring pro baseball back to Delaware.

Cratty wasted little time and quite a bit of type in a column exposing the deal as little more than a quid pro quo, noting that the state commission chairman had access to more than enough funding to front such a project on his own and thus avoid the city going on the hook. Local officials and promoters, among them members of the Daily Call's management, must have thought it was no big deal repaying the team owner who had done such a big financial favor for the city's economic rebirth.

The hitch was, city fathers had to go to local voters to get permission to undertake bond debt and request what was assured as a "slight" property tax increase.

At yet another stop, in Cratty's career, he drew the ire of a city's power structure by means of his column. The bond issue predictably failed, as those without the bank accounts to get in on the ground floor of this investment opportunity and taxpayers came down solidly against the effort.

Another member of the staff, a business writer, was publicly pilloried for a similar stance expressed in news articles on the deal. The main complaint emanated from the promotional group pushing the stadium, which just happened to have among its membership the newspaper's then publisher.

Cratty ran the exact same course every day, well at least five days each week. He'd head just a block west in an alley off 17th Street to Locust. From there, he'd turn south on Locust until it merged with Bluff, a one-way that would take him in front of his place of work – The Daily Call – in downtown.

He could run the circuit in his sleep. And sometimes, for all he remembered of the trip, he probably did.

He'd continue south, sticking to the west side of the street until First Street where he'd keep south to Bluff's outlet to Dodge, a main east/west artery that served as the route east over the Mississippi.

Then he'd do two loops of the block before continuing an easterly jog in downtown along Main Street.

From there it was a zigzag making his way back north to his apartment.

The entire course covered just over three miles, meaning he'd worked his weekly limit back up to the 15-mile range.

It had taken him the better part of the last six months to get back into running this much, and he had those same old aches and pains he remembered from his road racing days in the 1980s to prove it.

While he was in New Mexico, he found that running at altitude proved a little more than he could handle. So, the running in Delaware was a whole new lease on life.

Cratty started the running kick when he was going through his first divorce and decided to give up smoking two packs a day. He'd worked himself up to almost six miles shortly after reaching Michigan.

Running always seemed to clear his mind, and since it was always done just after rising in the morning, it seemed to set the pace for the rest of his waking hours.

That's why he noticed that something was wrong when he couldn't get back out on the road following back surgery in 2009.

He'd been laid up for several months at the end of 2009 with a herniated disc. An orthopedic surgeon solved the problem but advised him to confine his workouts to treadmills.

He soon found a gym and was back up to two to three miles per day in the spring of 2010.

Then the coughing started.

"Cratty, it's for you," announced the receptionist when he picked up the phone at his desk at the far end of the newsroom.

It was the doctor he'd been seeing – a pulmonologist he'd consulted about the cough. The guy had found what he described as a mass that looked like shards of broken glass in his left lung. There was a biopsy done after all the other possibilities were eliminated, and the doctor was calling with the results.

"Pat, I'd like to set up an appointment, so we can discuss the results of the biopsy," said the doctor, using the kind of tone that denotes less than happy tidings.

"No, doc, you can spill it over the phone," answered Cratty. "I can tell that it's not good news."

"Pat, I'm afraid it's cancer. You've got bronchioloalveolar carcinoma."

You never get around to thinking about just what you're gonna say when somebody in a white coat tells you you've got cancer. He was almost numbed by the moment. For just a moment, he even thought he was being some sort of hero by keeping up the front while awaiting the news.

It didn't really register at first, and Cratty initially thought he had two different kinds of cancer from the number of syllables involved.

According to the pulmonologist, it was a rare form of cancer, most usually found in "20 to 40-year-old, nonsmoking Asian women." His bent toward newsroom humor immediately referenced Viet Nam and the last time he'd ever had intimate contact with that type of female.

For a moment, he considered how he might even be able to wangle a Purple Heart, but it was a fanciful flight and he immediately dismissed the idiotic idea.

The humor didn't last long.

Several years later, he would discover that the illness was indeed connected to his stint in Southeast Asia, but not to any extracurricular activities.

It was Agent Orange.

Just short of 50 years from Viet Nam, he would learn that he was another casualty of that war that he thought he'd long ago escaped without a scratch.

It would take another seven years for the VA to get around to considering some form of compensation for the cancer, and by then he'd have already surrendered his left lung in two separate operations and the malady had invaded his right.

A VA oncologist would eventually tell him what he already knew, "there is no treatment or possible cure."

Despite that fact, the VA seemed to feel that since he was still able to draw breath, no matter how little, it was not their responsibility.

Thank you, LBJ! It all felt a lot like his luck in the Army. Patriotism was beginning to be a word and/or concept far removed from Cratty's vocabulary.

Looking back, it all seemed a little stupid now.

It was the first time Cratty had ever heard shots fired in anger and at him.

Hell, at first, he and the rest of his outfit were so green, just a couple of weeks off the boat, they weren't even aware of the fact that they were under fire.

Just some firecracker like pops and a lot of confusion.

Somebody yells, "Get down!" and everybody scrambles for a little patch of real estate.

Complicating matters was the fact that the entire outfit was smack in the open, walking through some half-dried rice paddies at the base of a few hills on a battalion sweep just north and west of Cam Ranh Bay.

The 1st Brigade had disembarked from the USS LeRoy Eltinge at Cam Ranh earlier that month – long before the deep-water port would be built up into one of Southeast Asia's busiest. The brigade had come ashore in landing craft earlier in the month and this was little more than an exercise getting the paratroopers used to the climate, for Christ's sake.

Cratty is humping the M-60, and a Mexican kid from just outside of Phoenix is toting the ammo. They both hug the ground, which is in the semi-solid mud stages between rice seasons.

As Cratty sprawls spread eagle, with the machine gun over his right shoulder, he hears something akin to a bee buzzing near his left ear. He turns quickly to see what the sound is and notices a narrow rut dug into the mud starting about his ear and running under his shoulder and down the entire left side of his body.

He doesn't know it then, but that's as close as he would come to having his number called during his tour in 'Nam. Oh, he had moments when he got white-knuckle scared, for sure, but that .30-caliber round in the mud just an inch or two past his ear and under the left side of his body, was as close as they ever came.

"Cratty!" shouted Sgt. Davis. "Get some fire on the side of that hill to the front."

Having a few rounds already hanging in the M-60, Cratty, without even bothering to unfold the bipod struts, shoved the gun out in front of him like he's feeding it on a line.

He leaned into the butt and squeezed off a burst, taking care to make it short.

"Cratty!" screamed Davis, this time a few octaves higher. "You fuckin' idiot. What are you tryin' ta' do? Kill me?"

In his rush to "get some fire" on the hill, Cratty had forgotten that Davis was lying almost directly in front of his position, and his initial burst was going right over his platoon sergeant's head.

Later in life, those rounds would get closer and closer to Davis' head with each telling of the story.

"Get the fuck up here!" screamed Davis.

So, disregarding the situation and seemingly in a fog, Cratty simply stood up, walked the four feet or so to where Davis was huddled against the damp earth, and laid back down, ready for action.

"You are fucking amazing Cratty," Davis said later. "Besides being the biggest fuck-up it has ever been my misfortune to come across in this man's Army, you gotta be the luckiest."

It was something Davis never let him forget, as Cratty was always the first member of the platoon Sarge would "voluntell" for anything the rest of their tour in 'Nam.

That's most likely the reason the call to battalion headquarters at Fort Bragg on that day his last year in the Army would confuse him so much. It had to be the leavings of another predicament that Davis had "voluntold" him for.

It's strange how reactions to life-threatening situations are, in many instances, delayed.

After the shooting had stopped and the guy behind the offending weapon, whoever he might have been, had long since moved on to other targets of opportunity, Cratty felt that "hot flash" starting deep in the pit of his stomach and then spreading instantaneously to every nerve ending. Then he got violently ill. He threw up for a half hour and then when he had nothing left to add, started in with the dry heaves.

For the rest of his life, he'd be able to quickly conjure up that immediate hot flash that always accompanied danger – and then that sudden urge to be physically ill – every time he felt threatened.

And he will never forget the sound from that film clip of his life. Charlie was using a B.A.R. (Browning Automatic Rifle), an old, World War weapon, and it sounded like a 105-Howitzer on semi-automatic.

The only thing that Cratty could figure about the bizarre incident was that the guy on the shoulder end of the B.A.R. was as stunned by Cratty's absent-minded maneuver as everyone else on the field that day, and he just didn't have the heart to shoot the idiot and put him out of his misery.

He'd almost missed it. In the daydreaming that usually accompanied those mesmerizing drives that are always a part of midsummer Illinois, he almost forgot just where he was. But as he made the long lazy turn just past Roanoke

Road, swinging along the railroad tracks, he could see the grain elevators rising like skyscrapers out of the six-foot-tall corn about a half-mile north of the highway.

There he was, once again sitting beside the road just past the turnoff that goes into what there is of Melvin. That nameless face who was there many days and just seemed to be staring right past the traffic whizzing by on the two-lane highway.

Cratty couldn't help but feel that this apparition, which he'd seen any number of times over the early 1990s, was placed directly in his path. Like someone was still trying to send him a message and he couldn't quite get it.

Just what in the hell did this nameless and probably unstable stray road guard from a long-gone parade know that Cratty did not?

It was an almost surreal scene.

A full battalion of paratroopers passing along Highway 1 on the Vietnamese coast while an old woman, stripped completely naked, stood on a cement kilometer marker along the roadway screaming at the top of her lungs.

"Road guards out," came the command, and the two troops at the front corners of the formation would run out and stand at parade rest in the intersection halting the cross traffic.

Nobody understood a single word she was saying, at least none of the Americans in the audience. Cratty certainly didn't catch any of her drift. Outside of getting a meal, a beer or laid, he couldn't speak a word of Vietnamese.

But he'd remember till the day he died that old woman without a stitch of clothes standing beside the highway shaking her fist at the passing paratroopers.

And perhaps the strangest part of the incident was the fact that nobody, especially among the military personnel in the group, seemed to take any notice of the withered old hag, tits drooping to her knees and skin hanging like a loose sheet.

He was certain that he wasn't the only one who'd seen the old woman as he stood road guard at one of the intersections. But nobody, at the time or throughout the rest of their tour in 'Nam, ever mentioned it.

He wondered at that moment how many other guys, and there must have been hundreds that day, still had that bizarre scene trapped inside their heads.

And, just like the guy he saw beside the road near Melvin, Cratty got the distinct impression that that old woman knew something he didn't.

That was the last time Cratty had the same feeling he did looking at the stranger beside the road in Melvin.

Was this guy nuts, or was he? What secrets was he keeping? Just like that old naked Vietnamese woman beside a similar road 30-some odd years earlier.

12. Fairy-Tale Ending

"I've gotta get outta this business," he told his first wife just a month into his second job back in 1972. "I think the guy working the desk in the sports department on weekends hates me."

He really did live in fear of being fired for what might be the simplest of mistakes early in his career, but he soon discovered that mistakes, if they weren't fatal, were the best learning experiences.

"In somebody's newspaper today, there will be a story about a guy being robbed at a drop deposit box last night," boomed Cratty's LaMotte managing editor.

"But not in mine!"

He was looking squarely at Cratty as he walked slowly across the newsroom; Cratty, the rookie whose job it was each morning to check the LaMotte Police Department night log for just such bits of information.

He'd only been on the job, his first, a couple of months in the winter of 1970-71. He'd fucked up big time. In perusing the log that morning Cratty had missed the biggest cop item in town in months.

That was the first time he'd escaped termination for utter incompetence. And it was the day he learned that the profession is picked up one mistake at a time.

He'd make lots of them before hanging it up in 2015, but there was no other way to earn your byline.

Unlike these kids populating the Delaware newsroom in the 21st century, you never put your own byline on a story back then. That was the job of your editor or somebody on the news side city desk.

And when you finally did get that byline, it was cause for celebration.

He still remembered when his dad called from back home – about 50 miles from where he got his first break with a major daily – not long after he had finally gotten one of his first bylines, complaining that he was "Pat Cratty" and that his son's professional moniker should be "Pat J. Cratty."

That was the first time he realized that not only was his father reading his stuff but that he'd finally impressed the old man. And when he got into it with the bunch running the racetrack in 1975, Pop was more than just a little concerned.

"I don't think you understand that these guys are serious," his dad tried to warn him. Thank God, he never told him about the not-so-subtle threat he got during that episode.

That call from his father back in the Quad Cities ensured that his byline would always carry the "J." from that day on.

By the time Cratty got to Delaware, the time-honored practice of learning from your mistakes had taken on a much more serious bent.

Shortly after Cratty arrived at the Daily Call, the executive editor went on an obsessive kick about errors. And it turned out that his fetish wasn't with what you might call the most major fuck-ups. In fact, Cratty discovered his boss was obsessively fascinated with the mundane and minuscule examples of the practice.

Thus, the highest-ranking member in the newsroom chain of command insisted that these mistakes – misspelt words, names, wrong dates, time or place or screwed-up cutline – were tantamount to capital crimes.

Now, most veterans in the business will tell you that while such foul-ups were extremely annoying, they were unavoidable. But at the Daily Call, these mistakes were to be meticulously tracked and recounted at monthly staff gatherings with the use of painstakingly crafted graphs and charts.

And, to ensure the message was getting through, each and every one was to be recounted on the paper's front page.

Of course, the number of such mistakes never seemed to show any signs of decline. And all the practice did was to take up valuable time and space in the paper's computer mailboxes, as the person designated to keep track had to send a chain email around the newsroom for the explicit purpose of having anyone connected with the error, from perpetrator to proofreader, explain his or her precise excuse and display the proper contrition.

The boss used, as a defense of the anal-retentive practice, a line he remembered from a long-lost seminar he'd once attended. According to this scripture, "The greatest fear in any newsroom is the fear of being wrong."

To say the man had seriously misunderstood the warning contained in that admonition was quite an understatement. Because Cratty had heard the exact same proscription from the author of the idea, and knew that that "greatest fear" had nothing whatsoever to do with mere misspellings, transposed dates or misbegotten cutlines. While such fuck-ups are and always have been an industry problem, the fear arose from a much more profound consideration. It had everything to do with being wrong when it came to the facts of a given story, which was a mistake that didn't seem to, much bother the same man in the corner office.

Cratty finally got around to marrying Sarah, his fourth wife in the late spring of 1999 when he was out West, flying back to Illinois on a short week's vacation to tie the knot (fourth marriage for each) in a private ceremony in a retired minister's living room.

The living arrangements were a little awkward, but it'd turn out to be the best relationship of Cratty's life.

It would always be a long-distance marriage, and the two of them soon got used to it. In fact, they never actually lived in the same home throughout their married life.

It was during his fourth wife's first visit out West that Cratty had the "shit down your neck" run-in with the lunatic he worked for.

Cratty loved New Mexico, and if not for the crazy publisher, he could have finished his career there. But then his new wife was not impressed with the Southwest, where she thought there were far too many rocks and not nearly enough green.

There was also something about the Native American culture that Cratty found appealing. In fact, he applied for and came very close to getting the job as editor of the Hopi Indian Nation newspaper. But once he told the wife that the accommodations in a 400-year-old village atop a mesa in northeast Arizona had the only electrical hookup within 50 miles, that was the end of that.

Shortly after making the regular column roster at Delaware, Cratty was tabbed to fill in writing editorials while the usual author took a vacation.

He remembered it because it was right around the time of the traumatic events of September 11, 2001.

One of his first offerings centered on a local Chamber of Commerce screw-up regarding the start of work on the Ice Harbor tourism project. It was something over a week since the national tragedy and involved somebody's fucked-up idea to celebrate the event with a 9:00 a.m. fireworks display along the Mississippi Riverfront in downtown.

Of course, the racket set off mass hysteria, as schools, stores and production plants in that part of town were scrambling for cover. The city's alternative high school, just a quarter-mile from the noise, began sending students to the building's basement, setting off the alarm system.

Cratty likened the stupidity to Hollywood's comedic "1942," when Los Angeles is thrown into complete chaos when a Japanese submarine shows up off a Southern California beach within weeks of Pearl Harbor.

The piece was more comic than caustic, but it was the last time he'd pen an editorial for the Daily Call.

The reaction from the bean counters was something like, "We realize how stupid this stunt might appear in retrospect, but we'd rather not ridicule the city hierarchy over the matter."

Once again, Cratty had arrived and placed himself squarely between his superiors and what he always believed to be the sacred duty that accompanied his profession as he saw it.

Things would get worse.

"Hello, Rebecca," he said after realizing who was on the line.

"I hadn't heard from you in a while and wanted to know how things were going," she began, much like she always began.

He hadn't talked to her in almost a month, and that was unusual. It showed an amount of emotional control he didn't think he possessed.

This woman had always had a mesmerizing hold on him. It was so obvious that he had started regretting it over the last four or five years. Before that, he was just as enthralled with the sound of her voice and totally captivated by the woman as he'd been when he was the 15-year-old kid feeling his way through the first real sparks of love back in high school.

Maybe the fact that her mother – it was actually her stepmother – couldn't stand Cratty and liked even less the idea that the eldest girl in the family was involved with a boy from the south side of town that proved as much of a fuel for the relationship as anything you'd call love.

The "south side" of the town was where all the Irish and Mexicans hailed from, the descendants of those immigrants who'd built the railroad in his home county, for a long time the biggest industrial power within many miles. Of course, the railroad was long since built by the time Cratty – a fourth-generation second-class citizen came on the scene.

His grandmother Harriett's generation had helped start the strong railroad union movement of the 1910s and '20s and he had the feeling that Rebecca was simply the product of a class of people who would never forgive them for it.

Whatever the reason for the obstacles placed in the path of this young romance, Cratty always seemed to exaggerate the situation. He probably always saw himself as the kid from the wrong side of the tracks, which he was, continuing the struggle for equality and social recognition begun by his Grandma Harriett and the Paden boys, two of whom had to end up finding careers in the military after being "blackballed" out of railroading for their union activity.

"Mr. Paden," boomed a judge from the imposing bench of a federal courtroom in about 1925, "it's been alleged that you called your fellow workers 'Scabs, scabby asses and scabby ass sons of bitches?'"

Ralph Paden – the youngest of Grandma Harriett's nine siblings – immediately shot back with: "Yes, Your Honor, and they are scabs, scabby asses, and scabby ass sons of bitches."

Of course, that unorthodox legal defense ended in a contempt of court citation and sent Uncle Ralph on a 30-plus-year career in the United States Army.

Cratty even considering a stint in the Army was a direct result of his determination to prove himself "good enough" for Rebecca's parents. He was just foolish enough to really believe that he and she were destined to be together and that, like the prince versus the evil stepmother in Cinderella, he'd find a way to place that glass slipper on her foot. However, he wasn't quite as sure just how he'd ever become the prince in the story that does the placing. He still had to work that part out.

And a fairytale prince would be exactly what it'd take to pull off this trick.

But in recent years, he'd come to discover that the obstacles of class between them weren't all of her parents' making. He now knew that much of the wide distance between them was just as much the product of her upbringing and that his awkward courage would never be enough to carry his white steed over the fissure.

"I guess I'm just not the risk-taker you are in our relationship," she had said in an attempt to explain why she was ending this latest installment of their more than 30 year relationship in the fall of 1990, when he had been laid off in Texas and was about to finally move back to Illinois.

Perhaps it was the prospect of that move that had caused her to succumb to the advances of an older man who was a retired executive and had lived, before his own divorce, just a few doors down.

Whatever it was, the relationship, at least the intimate part of it, came to an end as quickly as it had begun just before he returned to find work in Illinois.

Ironically, the two, despite 25 to 30 years of supposedly being "in love," had never been intimate until they'd drifted back together in the late 1980s.

He guessed that she felt safe in taking the relationship to that level as long as he was still living 900 miles away in Texas.

Part of the reason for the continued contact was the relationship he'd built up with her two daughters. The younger would always refer to Cratty as her "second dad." And, when the final breakup came in the fall of 1990, the two girls put up quite a fight, trying to convince their mother she was making a mistake.

Who was he kidding? He had no choice in the continued connection. He'd have talked with her no matter what.

He continued, fool that he was, to cling to that dream that someday she'd see that God had always intended them to be together, chuck this old man she was engaged to and they'd live happily ever after.

Of course, he was always unable to explain all this to the ever-practical Rebecca. She was one of those individuals who always know the right thing to either do or say. She certainly wouldn't let emotion play a role in what she did with her life.

So, the pleasure/pain romance would drag on for almost three decades after going their separate ways in the winter of 1990. But by then, it was mostly carried on over the telephone in calls she usually initiated. By 2010, Rebecca had married the retiree and continued to live in Illinois, spending winters in Florida.

In the spring of 2015, Rebecca placed her last call to Cratty, who was by then about to retire.

He remembered the call distinctly. She was on her way driving north up the west coast of Florida to Tampa-St. Pete for one of her grandson's sporting events.

As usual, she was driving and talking on her car's cell phone, a practice Cratty believed she followed so as not to have to call when her husband was around.

Like most of the phone calls between them in recent years, Cratty was only about halfway into the conversation. He answered all the questions and was good with uninvolved small talk, but it was like something deep inside had a chokehold on his participation.

He should have paid closer attention.

Less than two weeks later, Cratty returned from work late one night in early March to find a Facebook message from Rebecca's stepsister, Julie, who lived in the Pacific Northwest and was insisting that he call.

What startled him most about the message was that it was from someone in the family he never remembered being especially fond of him. So, of course, he knew it was something he didn't want to hear.

"Jake," she began with her voice noticeably cracking, "I had a terrible time running you down. I never knew your first name was Patrick.

"Rebecca," she continued, by this time fighting back tears and not bothering to segue into the shock, "is on life support."

It all came crashing down so quickly, he was in a state of shock, feeling numb and devastated all at the same moment. He couldn't recall having anything like that feeling since returning from 'Nam almost 50 years earlier.

"What?" he asked, not actually needing her to repeat herself, but as more of a reflex-like when one wakes up from a bad dream.

"She suffered a stroke in her sleep down in Naples and wasn't found until early this morning. They've put her on life support in Florida until her daughters and another sister can get there."

Cratty immediately erupted in a foul-mouthed explosion, dulled just a bit by absolute confusion and an uncontrollable urge to punch a hole in his apartment wall.

"Goddamn, this can't be happening," he said after he finally got command of his powers of near civil speech. "I just talked to her not more than two weeks ago."

"Evidently, she had a severe headache and went to bed early last night," Julie tried to explain. "Her husband came in to check on her and urged her to go to the emergency room, but since she's always had bad headaches and you know how she is, she refused and tried to sleep it off."

"The next morning, he found her in bed."

Cratty didn't know what to say or do. He wanted to break down and cry, and he was hit by a feeling of uncontrollable anger. He also went back to their last phone conversation trying desperately to reconstruct it and hating himself for being so goddamned distant.

This could not be happening. This was the woman that GOD had ordained as the love of his life. And even though he knew, deep down inside, that all that was bullshit, he was almost choking for his inability to catch his breath on the verge of tears.

And then he was so mad at himself. Ever since the breakup in 1990, Cratty had laid the blame on her for being too class and material conscious and that that was the root of the problem.

He then was overcome with a complete sense of shame for not seeing that the love of his life had been so right one more time.

He'd finally discovered that, like most every other time in their fits and starts, Rebecca always made the right decision. His journeyman career in newspapers was not conducive to a woman with two teenage daughters. Traipsing from one end of the country to the other with a self-possessed newsroom junky in search of God knows what kind of security was not in the cards.

Cratty eventually came to accept the wisdom of his childhood sweetheart, but it would come much too late to help either of them now. She was right, and like most of those instances in their past, it drove Cratty crazy because and especially owing to the fact that he never got the chance to tell her so.

Hell, Cratty's first marriage to Catrina, which resulted in the two daughters who were the heart and soul of his existence, wouldn't have survived his newspaper-to-newspaper lifestyle any better.

The breakup with Rebecca in 1990 hit him hard, probably a lot harder than he knew. For several years after that, Cratty even refused to drive through the town she once lived in on the interstate, preferring to use the extra 20 miles or so of a four-lane bypass on his frequent trips to his various jobs in eastern parts of Illinois, Indiana, and southwest Michigan.

That was foolish, and that insanity was now magnified by Rebecca's death.

"You know I worry about you," she had often said on the phone or face-to-face. And now it was her who should have been the one he and everybody else had worried about. And he also realized that he'd have to latch on to an entirely different fairytale for the rest of his life. Because he was suddenly ejected from this one.

From that day on, Cratty was truly mad at the God he thought had so horribly deceived him. He was initially outraged and then overcome with disgust for the concept of a supreme being.

There was no God, and he'd pissed away more than 50 years of his life on superstition and mystic children's stories.

He'd actually refused to ever think of Rebecca sexually when he was a teenage boy, who should have been obsessed with nothing else at that age. Oh, he still exhibited all the requisite physiological responses in those very few times they ever got to actually "make out," as they used to say. But that and long walks home bent over at the waste with a wrenching gut ache was all that ever came of the activity.

He had never once ever allowed himself to so much as masturbate thinking of the girl that God had ordained for him. And, he felt more than just a little psychologically weird about that fact later in life.

Oddly or perhaps understandably, when they finally did get around to the intimate part of the love affair – almost 30 years and a couple of marriages too late, when they were both in their 40s – that peculiar sexual proscription and/or taboo would cause more than a few problems for him.

But he also felt bad for all the relationships he'd shattered in pursuit of what he was once sure was divine providence.

And chief among those he'd completely abused and misused in this tragic soap opera was his first wife and two daughters. But, much like that afternoon near Tuy Hoa, it was something he couldn't ever make up for now, and he was filled with self-loathing because of it.

He owed Cat a debt of gratitude he could never repay. She was and is a fantastic woman. She made up for the fact that Cratty was not only an absent father, but a self-centered asshole as well.

His career always came first. It was either the newspaper he was at or the one he was looking to find next that occupied Cratty's existence. And, if not for the fact that his first wife shouldered the chores and rewards of raising two little girls from infancy to womanhood that career never would have happened.

Come to think of it, he owed two grown women an apology as well.

Perhaps the real irony of the story was the fact that a career spent building a reputation for speaking truth to power was a sham.

In the end, that would be the toughest thing to live with.

Because as much as he might try to tell himself otherwise, he too had something to be horribly ashamed of about that day in a field near the Song (River) Ba, where several young men came face-to-face with their first test of humanity and failed badly.

Some because they had a sick rage inside that came to the surface in the chaotic circumstances of war. And the rest because they just weren't brave or man enough to stand up for and display their own humanity.

And even though Cratty had spent almost every day since that hot afternoon speaking up, he could never run away from the one time he did not.

He had never once, in 30 years in the newspaper business, ever sat on a story. So, he was bound and determined he would not sit on this one too much longer.

187

13. Girl on a Bridge

Cratty would put an end to his column-writing career long before he bid farewell to a newsroom. It came after one of his pieces, the last of his official offerings in The Daily Call was turned down by his executive editor. It certainly wasn't the first time one of his epistles had been rejected, but for him, it was the last time.

"Pat, I can't run this," said the man who had probably been most responsible for his being hired at Delaware in the first place. They had met while both were in college, well he was a freshman and Cratty was a newly minted journalist at LaMotte, just outta State.

"What's the problem?" quipped Cratty either not registering the statement at first or thinking it was a joke.

However, the man issuing the orders was not known for his sense of humor, so it was more likely Cratty was simply not paying attention.

"This countermands my front-page apology!" the boss continued without a breath.

The rather convoluted chain of events leading up to this confrontation began almost a month earlier. But more accurately, for Cratty at least it was something that had its beginnings in an incident he'd witnessed just months after his arrival in Delaware back in the summer of 2000.

Sometime in the spring of about 2008, the Daily Call's senior photographer happened upon a very dramatic scene as a group of people stood around a teenage girl who had managed to get around the safety fence on a bridge almost 50-feet above a four-lane highway running through the center of town.

The youngster was threatening to jump, and law enforcement officials had shut down traffic both ways on the major thoroughfare.

A woman was trying to hold the girl's hand through the chain link fence and she and at least one policeman were trying to calm the young lady and bring her in off the ledge.

Daily newspaper photogs are always out and about looking for feature pics to fill the pages of local publications. It's a widespread practice.

Well, this particular shot – one of several taken at the scene – went on the front page of the next morning's Delaware Daily Call.

As could be expected, there was an immediate uproar in the community, claiming that the paper had invaded this young woman's privacy and that it made the teen the object of undue ridicule, even though hundreds had witnessed the incident lasting more than an hour high above the busiest highway running through a town of almost 50,000 people.

Well, owing to the usual lack of backbone in both the newsroom and executive suites in the building, the next morning's edition contained a front-page apology for that picture.

Despite the apology, the photo was later submitted for a number of awards, which it garnered for both its spot news and emotional content, a fact that would later go unreported by the same paper now doing a front-page mea culpa for the dastardly deed.

Cratty waited almost a month after the picture's apology and then authored one of his twice-monthly offerings on the topic.

He harkened back to his first few months in town, a summer Saturday morning when he happened upon the body of a young man who must have jumped or perhaps was even pushed from the 100-foot bluff that rises just west of downtown and runs the entire length of the city north and south above the Mississippi River.

But readers of the Daily Call would never know what had really happened to the young man.

While out for his usual daily run, Cratty had come across a crowd of people near an intersection below the bluff near the city's public library.

One of those gathered around the apparent corpse, ran out, and asked if Cratty could tell if the young man was "dead."

Dead was something he knew a little bit about, having seen more than his fair share.

He could tell from quite a distance that the body was indeed lifeless and asked if the authorities had been notified. They had and after calming a couple of people at the scene, Cratty continued his run which went past the newspaper office, where he went upstairs to make sure the reporter charged with that morning's police beat was on the story.

When he finally got his column on the picture together, he concentrated on that earlier death, which he nor anybody else ever found out was a suicide or something more sinister. In fact, after the initial report of finding the body, not another word ever appeared, save a simple obituary that recounted little more than the young man's name, age, and family particulars.

The paper's policy, like most publications was not to publicize suicides outside of those committed in public.

Cratty wondered in print if that earlier story had been covered a little more aggressively, would the teenage girl have been standing on that ledge a few years later.

Was the 2000 incident a suicide and what might have caused a 19-year-old man who seemingly had a long, full life ahead of him to end things so painfully on the cold black pavement?

He also wondered if, the morning the bridge picture appeared in print, did any parents take a second look at the teenagers across the breakfast table? Did even a few consider that those teens might be coping with things their parents just couldn't begin to understand?

In his own way Cratty was doing what he believed was the first and only job of a credible newspaperman, telling readers what "THEY NEED TO KNOW" not just those things they may "WANT TO KNOW."

Like other near religious beliefs Cratty held in pursuit of his profession, Orwell had codified yet another: "If liberty means anything at all, it means the right to tell people what they do not want to hear."

But that would be a point of view Cratty would never get to present to the readers of The Daily Call. And it would be the last point he would ever make to them in print.

This was the same publication that made unholy fun of a man accused of murder and then ridiculed in 20,000 plus copies his family's final tribute in a vile editor's note attached to his obituary.

And now, Cratty's recounting of a local near tragedy in hopes of a teaching moment was a step too far?

It was certainly Cratty's final column in Delaware, but it did little to keep him from raging against the machine at virtually every aspect of that paper's newsroom.

It might have been his final epistle but later followed by many another instance of what Cratty believed were breaches of journalistic ethics by his employers.

Following a story by the paper's business writer, who simply pointed out that a local bank holding company, according to its own quarterly report, had experienced a financial loss, the paper got some heated calls from company execs. In a matter of hours, the paper's publisher and executive editor marched over to the firm's headquarters a few blocks from the paper falling all over themselves to assuage the concerns of the bankers.

Cratty was certain that the fact the publication was also heavily invested in or with the local financial firm had a lot more to do with the maneuver than anything of a truly journalistic nature. Ironically, the penitent patrol was most embarrassed by the headline that topped the story, which pointed out that the financials had "slumped." But they tried to tell the reporter, who by the way had nothing to do with the headline, they went to the financial institution to support her work. Now, that explanation made little or no sense, as such could be accomplished during the initial phone call.

The same business desk scribe also delved into the dealings of one of the town's bigger advertisers, a Midwest grocery chain with several locations in town. The point of the tale dealt with the purchase of another store's pharmacy records that was accomplished without the knowledge of those with prescriptions at the purchased store. The reporter had been put on to the story by at least one customer who was fearful of their prescription records being accessed by the new pharmacy.

The Daily Call couldn't run that story because "we have to approach these things on a case by case basis," according to those making such decisions.

If there is one thing in a newspaper's quest for a story that is anathema to the entire process, it is when publications approach the truth on "a case by case basis." That adds the element, where the truth is concerned, that said truth is determined by the effect it has on the vested interests of those involved.

If a big advertiser or connected official is afforded extra consideration in matters that might be less than advantageous or portray them in a less than favorable light, that is not journalism, that's public relations as Orwell so brilliantly once explained. And newspapers should never be in the public relations business.

The reporter working the pharmacy story was presented with the choice of scuttling the piece or possibly costing fellow reporters' their jobs if the grocery chain decided to pull advertising in response.

It would be virtually unheard of for anyone in the grocery business to pull print advertising. Where else would a grocer go to allow potential customers to peruse its wares?

It was a clear attempt by management to silence a reporter by means of an economic threat.

Sometime later, local city officials bent over backwards, some would say it was more frontwards, and used state and local tax incentives to attract a national computer company, who in the interest of cutting costs and a union workforce in New York had agreed to occupy several floors in the town's tallest building.

The 1,000 plus well-paying jobs supposedly created in the move were quickly filled by a host of foreign workers using special visas who were anything but "well-paid," further helping the firm's revenue stream. Come to find out, the 1,000 jobs were much closer to a few hundred less and the several floors originally leased were quickly reduced once the deal was completed.

However, once again the community's public watchdog had a host of excuses for why they just couldn't push such a story.

Now the point of these various tales is that the media industry and most specifically local newspapers – easily the great majority of those practicing journalism in this country – have degenerated into almost complete irrelevancy.

Their once watchdog status, which use to seem the absolute minimum for the proper function of a democratic society envisioned by the Founding Fathers, is now little more than the practice of pushing Pablum at the behest of advertisers and community political and social elites.

It's now more profitable to cheer the local Chamber of Commerce and their ilk than it is to keep a watch on organizations that most if not all the media's management are dues-paying members of. That's now the new norm in the business and certainly explains part of the decline of the local print industry.

What far too many fail to perceive is that a watchdog press is democracy's very cornerstone and the one thing that ensures the concept's survival. Without a free press, the founding fathers knew that a trusted and honest government could not exist.

However, it wouldn't be the less than courageous stance of his superiors and most of the rest of the industry that would finally tip the balance for Cratty.

It would be a story of four teens who were killed along a rural country road in the summer of 2014 that would finally start the chain of events that would extricate him from that newsroom desk he was once so sure he'd keel over at in the throes of a cerebral hemorrhage.

So, in a way, he would exit with more of a whimper than a cataclysmic explosion.

It should have been a slam-dunk of a story really. One of those assignments most young reporters earlier in Cratty's career would fight each other getting out the door to cover.

Despite the fact that many have the mistaken vision of reporters as hard-bitten, callous souls piling up society's so-called dirty laundry for the prurient interest of faceless readers and those perverts attracted to such things, modern day newspaper reporters are too prone to, being spoon-fed news releases from law enforcement/government entities or their hired "spokespersons."

Nobody works a regular beat anymore. There aren't enough live bodies in a newsroom these days to scare up a spare adjective let alone a real story. Too many young reporters, so used to putting their own bylines on stories that it's now just a quick click on the keyboard, are so satisfied with simply calling the local spokesman for canned crap and waiting for a call back they wouldn't know a story or source from their favorite candy bar in the breakroom.

And they couldn't stir up an interview without a tape recorder and/or smart phone. And forget the ability to dictate a story over any phone if their $12,000-per-year lives depended on it. They rarely even bother going to a scene, crime or otherwise, preferring to wait on the heavily fashioned, officialized and convoluted press release to do it for them or by the phone on their desks.

A good illustration of that point came one night when the police scanner lit up with a call for assistance at a local tavern. Seems the bartender had just kicked a drunk out of the establishment after the customer walked in with a zebra and parrot in tow.

According to the scanner, the man ordered a drink for the zebra, got belligerent when the guy behind the bar refused and was ordered out.

As the squad car arrived, the cop spied a vehicle trying to exit the parking lot with a man behind the wheel, a zebra seated beside him as co-pilot and a parrot on the driver's shoulder.

Now, the reporter who finally came across the tale on the nightly report at the copshop, returned to the newsroom and wrote a rookie-like piece about a run-of-the-mill drunk tank collar.

According to the story turned in at the copy desk, where Cratty was on duty, a man had been charged with public intoxication, attempted DUI and oh, in the fourth or fifth graph, there was a zebra and parrot in the suspect's car.

Cratty erupted in a roar of laughter. And after he regrouped, immediately began to rewrite the story.

It only took about 15 minutes, but Cratty's version opened with a lead:

"A drunk, a zebra, and a parrot go into a bar... Now you might think this the opening line of a joke.
It isn't!"

The reporter had already left the building, as is usually the case these days, so Cratty reconstructed the tale. The next day he pulled the reporter aside and informed him that "back in the day, Bud, you'd had to kill every other reporter in the room trying to get outta here to cover a story like that."

The piece, which was placed in an awards bundle later that year won a statewide award for the guy whose name was on the byline.

Cratty once asked a stunned room of young reporters how many of them had the home number of any of their sources. All he got was a fucking lame "Why would we want to call a source outside of business hours?"

When Cratty tried to explain that he never got any story worth telling from someone during office hours, he got a room full of blank stares. You'd thought he was speaking Chinese.

On a bright early August Saturday, four kids, 14-year-old incoming freshmen at a rural county high school were motoring down a paved country back road piled onto a small four-wheel utility vehicle.

It was the final day of a local town festival, one of those end of summer Midwestern gatherings with lots of food and craft booths and brightly colored bounce houses and face painting.

It certainly wasn't the best way for underage youngsters to be traveling on a county highway. But it was summer, weeks from the start of school and it was an otherwise bright Midwestern day.

As they approached an intersection in the road protected from either direction by stop signs, a farm truck pulling a loaded stock trailer barreled through the red octagon warning, smashing into the four boys without so much as a skid mark.

All four youngsters were immediately killed, and it wasn't long before county sheriffs' deputies, as well as a host of onlookers were on the scene.

For the readers of the Delaware newspaper and unfortunately for the rest of the news consuming public in the region, that would be all the tale they'd know for almost the next month.

Of course, there was a hastily gathered news conference provided by law enforcement with lots of hemming, hawing, "uhs," and incomplete sentences to fill up a good hour but with nothing really in the way of answers.

Joining the local publication were at least two eastern Iowa television stations but there was a surprising lack of inquiry on the part of all the media present. It was probably not unlike a first-year college journalism course, lots of fresh young faces and absolutely no instinct or talent in the room.

Cratty, who was doing his regular Saturday evening stint on the copy desk had already been alerted to the story by the time he'd come to work mid-afternoon.

He met one of the TV journalists as she came into the bureau office which was situated in the paper's newsroom. His 43 years of experience had already told him there was far more to the story than he'd heard and it didn't take him long to put two and two together and come up with three letters, "DUI."

The TV talking head passed Cratty's desk and turned into her enclosed office. He knew the woman, who was a talented broadcaster not long out of the University of Missouri's lauded school of journalism and was a good friend of the aged print journalist.

Sticking his head into her office, Cratty asked how it had gone.

"Cratty, it was horrible," she explained, lifting her head out of her desktop and visibly upset by the day's events.

"Did they say that alcohol and/or speed was not involved?" were the next words out of his mouth, not wasting any time with small talk and getting right to the point.

"Why, no," she answered in almost a question like response. "There was never any discussion of alcohol or speed. It never came up."

"You mean to tell me that a group of journalists from several outlets both print and broadcast were gathered at an accident scene with four fatalities in broad daylight, and not one of them bothered to ask if alcohol or speed was involved?

"Did the law enforcement officials at the scene bring up alcohol and/or speed as a contributing factor?" he continued without so much as a breath.

"No, they did not."

"I don't know anything about this crash, the people involved, or the physical circumstances, but every reportorial instinct in this old gray-haired man's body is yelling at me that the person behind the wheel of that farm truck was dead drunk."

Cratty's mind immediately traveled back to a newsroom early in his career. It was in the border region along the Mississippi between Iowa and Illinois. At the time, there was sort of a journalistic cautionary tale or bit of folklore that use to make the rounds back then about a fresh out of school reporter manning the Saturday night copshop beat two weeks before Christmas.

The "cherry," whose job was to fill in on the weekend to cover the police log for Sunday's a.m. edition, got a wave from the city desk transferring a call from a cop at a local hospital. Seems a child had just passed away following a particularly tragic holiday accident.

The rookie didn't realize just how tragic the death was until after being filled in by the visibly shaken policeman who'd accompanied the child and his mother to the hospital in an ambulance.

The child, not more than 4 or 5, had taken an ornament off the family tree and swallowed it. An emergency call was followed by a ride to the nearest hospital where the child died.

Owing to the shock of the situation was the fact that this was the first time the young journalist had covered any story, let alone by himself and under such circumstances.

The kid went about everything he could remember from journalism 101 and his professors' lectures back at school and started compiling all the sad details. But certainly, there was nothing in all his textbooks or lectures to cover this particular situation.

He interviewed the cop, several nurses and a doctor on the scene, and then sheepishly approached the family, which was of course of little more than superficial help as the Christmas nightmare was still registering.

After more than two hours at the hospital, the cub reporter returned to the newsroom and went to a desk and attached typewriter at the far end of the room where he spent most of the rest of an hour pounding away on an old manual Smith-Corona.

It was certainly the toughest story he had ever envisioned and though it was perhaps his first, just might be the toughest he'd ever come across.

Almost an hour of loud banging, cutting and pasting graphs together with a glue bottle and brush in an effort to try and get the most painful story to flow, he delivered the piece to the copy spike on the city desk.

The young reporter was actually somewhat pleased with himself, thinking he'd handled a very tough situation with some small amount of professional competence and dignity. Certainly, it was a story that few if any journalists had ever come across and he was confident he'd done his best.

About 15 to 20 minutes later, he heard the shrill sound of his name being yelled across the newsroom.

Almost certain that his gruesome task might have even earned him his first byline right out of the gate or at the very least, a job well-done pat on the back from the editor, he started across the wide space toward the call.

Halfway to the city desk, he was halted by a shouted question. He didn't catch it all at first, but the editor repeated himself in a much louder voice: "What color, rookie?"

Initially confused the cherry shot back in a much lower tone, "What color, what?"

"What color was the ornament," followed the request. "And, if you didn't ask, call the family and ask now!"

It was a legend he hadn't thought about in the almost 40 years since he'd first heard it. And he couldn't for the life of him remember just where, when or who had relayed it to him.

And one of the key parts of the story that also struck Cratty was the fact that without the help of a beat cop and the interference of a "police spokesperson" the tragic story was that much better.

He also remembered something else he learned in that earlier newsroom. He had an editor who used to go through his domain the middle of the afternoon and interrogate reporters he found sitting at their desks, convinced that if they weren't out on their assigned beats, they weren't worth the pitiful amount they were being paid.

His editor-and-chief of that time especially distrusted reporters with clean desks.

That lack of real details about the four kids' deaths would stand for weeks. And during the first couple of those weeks, the story was focused on something as far from the actual point as you could get.

It quickly turned into a lament of the placement of the rural stop signs in the county, as the farmer's family and friends were all too quick to come up with explanations and excuses filled with geometric angles and local topography.

That only increased Cratty's suspicions.

Here was a 20 to 30 something local farmer driving a road he must have been down a hundred times at high noon, running through a stop sign and plowing into a utility vehicle and slaughtering four totally unprotected teenagers. And his supporters were dragging local TV crews back to the scene of the incident every single day complaining about the size, line of sight, and placement of rural stop signs?

There were nightly 30-second clips on the tube dissecting the geography, road grade, and distance from the top of a hill and if warning signs were "too small" leading to the intersection.

Perhaps, it was just another example of Cratty's innate cynicism, a character trait so lacking in the business these days. But it had always been one of his best instincts, and he certainly had more than an old reporter's hunch there was a lot more to the story than was being foisted on the public.

14. The Rest of the Story

The rest of the story, as the broadcast catchphrase of right-wing radio icon Paul Harvey would have put it, came a little more than three weeks later, when county officials finally got around to charging the farmer at the wheel of the fatal vehicle for driving drunk and four counts of vehicular manslaughter.

Cratty, who had been ranting about the incident since that tragic Saturday, was wondering just why there wasn't so much as a word out of those usually assigned such work. It was almost like he'd been transported to a parallel universe and the death of four youngsters was almost a non-story.

When the story finally did hit the street, which was probably already well-worn around town by the time the media got hold of it, it was the classic example of an overly cautious legal system trying hard to cross all the "t"s and dot, all the "i"s safely inside a bubble out of public and media view.

However, certainly, more than a handful of the public was already aware of the situation, which left the media with a gigantic problem.

"When a community knows something you don't," Cratty tried to explain, "you've expended credibility as a newspaper that you'll never be able to retrieve." And that certainly seemed to be the case. The reading public eventually tunes you out when you find it easier to not rock the boat and stir the shit.

It was a story that Cratty's grandson (still in high school at the time) could have stumbled across in two hours.

The deputies arriving at the scene found open liquor containers and beer in the vehicle, and all three occupants were obviously intoxicated.

Once the driver had been removed from the truck and realized what he'd done, he broke down in tears, and begged officials to get him away from the scene.

He was then transported more than 25 miles to the county lockup, where he was held before being taken to a local hospital for a blood alcohol test.

And then, inexplicably, he was released from custody and nothing more was said above a legal whisper until the real story broke in late August and early September.

The first law in Cratty's rules of reporting had always been: THERE IS NO SUCH THING AS A SECRET! A secret is something only one person knows, and for all intents and purposes that is most likely more of a fantasy than a fact. And if more than one person knows, a reporter worth his press pass and notepad can find out.

As Cratty and any other newspaperman worth a damn saw it, "Just how many people must have known the basics of this fatal accident over the intervening hours, days, and weeks following the tragedy?"

Certainly, there were a number of law enforcement officers present at the scene, a good number of fire, ambulance and other emergency personnel, as well as the usual number of passers-by, who always gather in droves around such situations like flies on fresh shit.

Then we move to the county lockup, where the driver must have been logged in prior to the blood test and where many other individuals worked or circulated.

There were those working in the hospital in and around the lab and reception – as well as any number of random people in the hallways – who must have noticed a man either disheveled or in some state of distress being escorted by sheriff's deputies and most likely wearing handcuffs.

And for the next three plus weeks, nobody in the media knew a thing.

No one in attendance at the initial press conference bothered to ask if "alcohol or speed" were at fault, with the tip off being that officials purposely avoided saying they were not.

Now, that was what any editor, city desk occupant or cohort in Cratty's vast experience would have deemed "reportorial malpractice."

Like the "cherry" in the cautionary tale of Cratty's rookie servitude, all the questions, no matter how uncomfortable, were not being asked or even contemplated.

Cratty had learned the trade at the feet of men with fedoras and ink-stained hands, who cut their teeth on life. They didn't sit in a lecture hall listening intently to the sanctimonious rules of academic amateurs or pore over books on proper grammar. In fact, a goodly portion of those he heard laying down the law probably never went to college.

The only mistakes they ever worried about were the ones that come from being late to a story or letting it fall through the cracks, not from misspelt names, wrong dates, times and places.

One of his first managing editors, Forrest Kilmer, earned his reportorial reputation by sitting in a rented room for weeks on the upper floors of a downtown hotel where he could observe, through binoculars, the traffic crossing a toll bridge over the Mississippi River linking Iowa to Illinois. The object of the vigil was to try and match the toll revenue reported by bridge authorities to the actual number of vehicles using the span.

He ended up compiling evidence that someone had been siphoning off a healthy share of the tolls based on his rough daily count of autos going over the bridge and handing quarters to the guys manning the booth.

When the eventual story came together and was prominently placed atop the front page, Forry sent one of his understudies, another reporter, to the tollbooth with copies and watched for the chagrined response of those on duty.

The crack scribe and World War II combat paratrooper would later climb to the top of the publication's newsroom that dark Friday afternoon President John F. Kennedy was assassinated on a Dallas street. When everybody else around him was losing their collective heads, he single-handedly pulled that afternoon's and next morning's editions together and made sure the Quad Cities was not left out of the tragic loop.

The fact that "Forry" was a former paratrooper, probably had a lot to do with the fact that Cratty would end up being hired at the paper. It also probably contributed to his continued employment at the region's leading publication.

Cratty learned early to always take advantage of every edge you can get in the business from his five-year stint at the largest paper he would ever be associated with, as well as a knack for investigative journalism.

To this day, Cratty still doesn't understand why the DUI crash was the proverbial straw in his decision to retire. Perhaps, it was the moment he finally understood that the profession, now so fat and lazy from years of being spoon-fed only a fraction of the story, had left him so far behind and wandered off in a whole new and ethically confusing direction.

There were probably 40 or more people who had a piece of the crash story in hand, but nobody bothered to run it down. A story that was probably common knowledge in much of the county already, and the area's major newspaper didn't have a fucking clue or even the slightest interest in finding one.

No reporter was assigned in large part because there were barely enough staff members to cover the regular beats and feature stories.

There were a number of ways to trip over the story in any direction, but these days reporters were too busy waiting for a press release or a phone call to be bothered.

It was most likely then that he concluded he'd spent more than 40 years practicing a dying profession. And when he finally retired from that profession, he knew it was suffering from the delusion that the cause of that agonizing death was the ever-changing tastes and interests of the reading public.

However, since that retirement, he was now certain the demise was a clear case of suicide.

The readers didn't abandon the print medium because there wasn't enough color or white space on the page, contrary to what the bean counters kept insisting. They weren't yearning for a far less complicated kind of journalism, tailored to the happier and more feature-centric brand of news. No, the business abandoned them for the chance at bigger advertising profit margins and less hassle.

When your business model depends on the handouts of those you're supposed to be keeping an eye on, you've already swallowed the poison.

Readers went from being the object of the exercise, as they certainly had been throughout the history of a so-called "free press," to becoming an inconvenient labor expense that interfered with the real money-making operation down in the advertising department, only making sure that the readers were appeased by hitting their front porch with a paper by a certain time each day became much more important than the actual content of said paper.

After all, the circulation side of the business was more of a pain in the ass. It got to be too much work as well as too expensive to have to keep up with the delivery complaints and collections, not to mention the cumbersome work of actually having to deal with the general public.

Things were much easier when kids were paid nickels and dimes to push the product in their neighborhoods. Nowadays, adults who were no longer employees but "contractors," were handling two and three routes for a bit more but still meager wages and more importantly, no benefits.

The available amount now being paid, assures that the labor pool is being drawn from something less than the brightest bulbs in the box.

Readers simply are no longer a necessary consideration in the business. Thus, print journalism was finished being concerned about the poor slob scratching his ass and sucking down his morning coffee at the kitchen table.

So, it seems the business went from Woodward and Bernstein to Donald J. Trump in the little over 40 years Cratty practiced the profession. It went from servicing the reading public to filling the space around the ads with just enough tranquility to be able to pass as a newspaper instead of a shopper, the only difference being selling subscriptions versus sending it to everybody's mailing address.

The bean counters provided consummate proof of their lack of respect for readers just a couple of weeks before Cratty exited the business.

Management announced in August of 2015 that the paper's presses were being dismantled and the publication, in the interest of boosting the bottom line, would henceforth be printed 80 miles away. This, of course, would require a ridiculously early deadline. It was a clear example of just what the management really thought of its editorial content.

In fact, the a.m. edition – long working toward a midnight deadline – would now be put to bed (sent to press) by 9 p.m. weeknights and 10 p.m. weekends. That made it impossible to include most, if not all, the nightly sports scores, let alone anything remotely resembling the latest news.

They certainly didn't care what was contained inside the publication, other than ad copy. They were always thinking of the bottom line, so much so that they would have been just as happy to deliver their advertising in oceans of white space sans any editorial copy at all.

And just think of how much they could save by doing away with the newsroom, its obvious expense, and the added need to worry about stirring things up with controversy.

Of course, the Daily Call had already deep sixed the latest news by operating an a.m. newspaper on a p.m. schedule. The newsroom was only fully staffed, if you want to call a collection of five or six scribes fully staffed, between the hours of 8 a.m. and about 5 p.m.

Once the clock struck 5:00, all the news that was then available was all the news that was not only fit to print but would be printed. Everything that happened until the sun rose the next morning was left for dead.

It was the first time Cratty had ever worked at an a.m. rag where the newsroom wasn't full to capacity once the sun went down.

When the product was being put together, the newsroom floor was a ghost town except for the copy desk, where the pages were edited and assembled. That meant there was little or no contact between those actually constructing the newspaper and those who wrote the copy, except for the inconvenient late-night phone call.

At his final staff meeting before retiring, Cratty informed the paper's management at a building-wide gathering just what he thought of the so-called bold move into the publication's future.

"I don't know just who came up with this idea, but you might as well take this paper's entire sports department, pile it up in the middle of the newsroom, pour gasoline on the heap, and strike a match!" he proclaimed, which was greeted by more than just a couple of gasps in the crowded room.

Management countered: "People can get sports scores anywhere. We don't need to send writers out to get scores."

"That's perfectly true. And if your sports staff is worth anything at all, you're not sending them out to just get a score. And, you're also telling your readers in the same breath they can find everything else you have to offer, including advertising, someplace else. With this move, you're actually directing them to a competing media – the internet," he tried desperately to explain.

But as was always the case throughout his fight with management and their fawning yes men, it was like talking to a wall.

Suddenly, it hit him square in the face. This shit was no longer his battle. Cratty was getting the hell outta this rat race and all this crap was now somebody else's problem. Somebody else who'd have to sit in some stuffy conference room 40 years from now and hear the same fucking, unbelievable bullshit coming from the same idiots in suits who had no more use for newsprint than to wipe their collective asses. Money was the only paper they really cared about and as long as it kept coming in the front door, they weren't the slightest bit concerned what was being sent out the back.

And he could at that moment actually feel the weight of 44 years of trying to roll the same rock up a steep hill melt away.

The high-water mark of his chosen profession was almost the day he got into it, the early 1970s when a pair of spare beat reporters started an avalanche that would bring down a United States' president.

The day that happened, those in positions of power (the obvious targets of such work), especially those with money enough to mount a counterattack, closed ranks and developed an entirely new plan.

They seemed intent on putting into practice that which Orwell had so prophetically laid out in his finest work, *Nineteen Eighty-Four*: "Who controls the past controls the future. Who controls the present, controls the past."

It was simply a matter of extracting from the general population its history. Once each succeeding generation in this country arrived with the mistaken impression that the world began the day they were born, the mission was well on its way to being accomplished.

That's why the study of things like history and geography, civics and the like were much more palatable corralled into two-week segments under the umbrella of "social studies." It was doled out in minuscule amounts with little time or attention paid to those social and political movements responsible for the very benefits those succeeding generations were actually enjoying.

Thus, people of Cratty's generation were left to provide more than a bit of the actual color and context of history to newsrooms stocked and run by the generations suffering from this somewhat stunted education.

Perhaps the tumultuous 1960s and the chaos they provided served as a wake-up call – more like a nightmare – to the leaders of the so-called "Greatest Generation?" The street choking marches against the Viet Nam War and for civil rights led Cratty's father's generation to conclude that if opening young minds to the ideals of social progress led to such consternation, it might be time to construct a quieter kind of history.

On more than one occasion while he ran out the clock on his career on the Delaware copy desk, Cratty had to come to the aid of many a colleague in matters of historic accuracy.

It was a lot like having to tell your 10-year-old daughter that "No, the Bee Gees did not invent rock 'n' roll" and "Yes, Sir Paul McCartney was in a band before Wings!"

And, at about the same time that bean counters discovered there was a lot more to gain from those with the money to spend on advertising, society's watchdogs were chained to the wall, toothless in favor of an entirely new business model.

Those bean counters suddenly found themselves in the driver's seat when media organizations – especially newspapers – made the brilliant decision to trade readers for profits.

They simply did away with newspapermen as publishers and substituted them with circulation execs – paperboys in suits – and their equally dapper advertising types.

When the management stopped telling people what they should know and started pandering to the advertisers' and oligarchs' need to keep them uninformed and uninterested in their real predicament, those readers couldn't get to the exits fast enough.

The failure was not in our stars, it was in our surrender to the concept that newspapers were nothing more than "a business."

And those who had long been the targets of an aggressive press could finally show those readers that since the media was no longer stirring up the populace, the only thing wrong was the minority or immigrant who was taking your job, misappropriating your taxes or was the cause of everything that was ruining your world.

The profession Cratty had spent well past half his life practicing surrendered its credibility in the pursuit of profits. And the distance between what was true or false was worn down to nothing. There was no longer anyone to measure that distance.

During his 1971 to 1976 stint under Kilmer, Cratty once heard his boss tell about a business seminar he'd attended in Boston.

The then editor of the Omaha World was at the gathering and tried to explain that his publication spent thousands of dollars each month shipping a few copies of the paper all the way to the other side of Nebraska to counties along the Colorado border. Those in charge of the session, all business types and media academics, were absolutely appalled.

"Why would you spend that much money, much more than you were ever going to recoup?" asked one of the seminar's presenters.

"Because, we're the newspaper of record for the state of Nebraska!" was the comeback.

So, as Cratty now saw the writing on the wall, the morphing of journalism into just another mercantile exchange had begun long before he was compelled to give it up. And all it really took was placing those "appalled" bean counters in the publisher's chairs of most, if not all, of America's many hundreds of local newsrooms.

So now it seemed to have gone full circle. Newspapers had long since surrendered the moral and constitutionally protected high ground to bloodsuckers in suits. And when we needed it the most, real journalism wasn't around and no longer cared.

It was the start of the era of moral equivocation in the media, which wasn't really interested in informing the public discourse. Now the object of the exercise was entertaining instead of educating.

Just a year after Cratty had retired during a critical presidential election, media outlets of all types placed two completely opposite moral ideals and ethical viewpoints on the same plain.

One, the truthless world of a morally bankrupt reality TV star turned carnival barker. The other the morally battered and personality challenged leftover from an earlier generation of leadership long past its prime.

And, even though they might both be from the same generation, they were not of the same moral and ethical value. However, the talking heads and a generation suffering from a 140-character attention span were bound and determined to convince us they were.

The media immediately demanded a show, a circus to entertain and distract the population and attract ratings in pursuit of ad revenue.

Add in the already weakened credibility of the nation's financially co-opted news media, daily being pilloried as the "dishonest" and "lying" press as simply peddling fiction, and we shouldn't be all that surprised at the eventual outcome.

That's what happens when you make two diametrically opposed sets of values morally equivalent in the interest of simplifying the problem for the consumers and hiding behind the shallow defense of "objectivity." But that so-called objectivity was dictated by the media's absolute fear of taxing the customers' already confused minds.

That's also what happens when a vital segment of society – the press, both print and broadcast – argues with itself about the difference between the words "lie" and/or "falsehood." There is only one that fits concisely in a headline and specifically expresses the truth.

The process was accelerated by the need for media of all stripes to draw in the viewers and reading public with a sensational copy without stopping to consider its veracity and/or sanity. The message was no longer important or even moral. It was the show that mattered, and media outlets – especially print – were so gun-shy from years of trying to bend over backwards to prove their "objectivity," they didn't have the strength of character or courage to call out the carnival barkers for the liars they really were and are.

Thus, the population mistook the media's fascination with the crude and outlandish for the reasoned and acceptable. Add to that the effect of the internet, a medium long misunderstood but fascinating to the mainstream media, and you have a perfect storm for the chaos that ensued.

On the internet, you needn't ever hear points of view that challenge your own, you simply click on to another catchy page that reinforces your already misinformed beliefs and petty prejudices.

Then we find that some, for their own nefarious purposes, put their fingers on the scale to make sure our deepest prejudices were fed a steady diet to cover the deception.

It's just a short hop from there to being portrayed as "FAKE NEWS" and being left with little or no defense for the charge.

We are then left with no more than two or three major newspapers in this nation even engaged in the business of trying to discern the truth at present and a bunch of talking heads yelling at each other from both extremes of the political divide on the nation's airwaves and passing it off as balanced.

This they portray as unbiased, disregarding the fact that absolutely nothing can be heard above all the shouting, and the public is left to rely on its own self-interest, prejudice, and the morally degenerate internet.

At his farewell gathering in late August of 2015, Cratty left his audience comprised mostly of rookie reporters and young editors with the cautionary tale of the cherry weekend cops' reporter, stuck on the desk two weeks before Christmas. But despite the tears, the story elicited he was certain that few if any in the room picked up what he was trying to impart. Finding the truth in the newspaper business is sometimes painful, sometimes uncomfortable, and very often hard.

But it's the only thing that matters.

It seldom has a truly happy ending, but it usually has a very important one.

Within a year of the day that he said goodbye to journalism, the most chaotic presidential campaign in American history was well underway, and the nation was headed for what he believed was certain doom.

Oddly enough, 2016 was the first presidential election night Cratty had not spent in a newsroom since 1968.

And, looking back, he was glad this time, even thankful he missed it.

At the time, we had yet to learn the horrifying facts of Russia's interference in the most sacred act of a democratic society: a free and fair election of its leaders. And since, we must wrestle with the fact that that interference has not and probably will never end.

From the way the matter is being treated by our current government – duly elected or not – there is no indication that we will ever be free of this plague.

What will happen when the next national balloting ends in an even bigger catastrophe, leaving our citizenry without an ounce of faith in its outcome?

And a democratic process without trust in the outcome is not a democracy, no more than is that practiced in Russia and any number of other kleptocracies anything other than totalitarianism.

The way things are going at the moment, that could well be the final eulogy for this and every other democracy, and those in this world preaching against its benefits and values will be the only ones left to pick up the pieces.

Suddenly, his mind went back to an almost forgotten stack of papers, buried in one of the many boxes he'd accumulated over the previous 40 years of moves from one mid-size newspaper and one-bedroom apartment to another.

It was a poem he'd fiddled with years earlier, and suddenly he sat down and finally put it all together. Outside putting his hand to any number of sarcastic rhyming missives of no great value that he was known for over the years, Cratty thought he'd left his more serious poetic attempts hidden under decades of journalistic cynicism.

However, he was beginning to lose his connection to the country he'd once been so anxious and proud to risk his ass for. Those feelings were quickly ebbing right along with the love he'd once had for his chosen profession.

It now seemed that the word "patriotism" was beginning to have a very hollow sound to it.

As the new century was headed toward its third decade, America was embarking on a very bad dream. Very few bothered to separate the concepts of "patriotism" and "nationalism." In fact, it now appeared the two words were dangerously interchangeable.

And that thought was beginning to eat at Cratty's guts. Finally, the poem he'd almost forgotten about simply fell into place:

'Nam Vet's Lament

America the beautiful, home of all that's brave, all we'll ever ask back from you is everything we gave. All the fervor that we shed, all the dreams of youth, all the lessons we were taught, lies that passed for truth.

For old men's honor we marched off, caught up in your schemes. Drop by drop, lives spilled out on your TV screens. We came home one by one, in the dark of night, as if you thought our deed so foul it shouldn't see the light.

Welcomed home those left behind but never those you sent, preferring sons of privilege to the souls you spent. A generation lost for good, diseased and left disgraced. We traded lives and sanity for the nightmares we now chase.

It seems the only lucky ones are the names that you recall. Those chipped and chiseled upon a long black granite wall. But our unknown soldier walks erect, no grave to rest his head. A million copies wandering with only spirits dead.

I no longer want what you want, believe what you believe. I don't know what it is that caused us all to be so deceived. Give us back our dreams, our arms, our legs, and honor left behind. But most of all, please give us back our minds.

The sun has set on this nation you seem so proudly to profess. There's so much you made of it that's now so much less. If I'd have known all of this some 50 years ago, the American dreamer I was then would have stood to tell you NO.

I didn't risk my life for you or the twisted dream you cling to now. So, you could tell me just where to stand and how. Or just what it takes to be American and showing pride. For as we all know, that's where all you scoundrels hide.

15. (30)

It took more than 20 years to piece together, but Cratty had finally finished that one book they say is in each of us. He was certain of that because he couldn't imagine anybody else in this life with that fucked-up a story to tell.

And its completion required just one more confession to tie the entire process together.

It was the toughest conversation he'd ever contemplated with the two women who were easily the most important in his life: his daughters.

The encounter was certainly more of a confession than a discussion, but either way, with or without the confessional's sliding doors and screens, it was an interaction Cratty had dreaded for decades. It had seemed to hang over the grizzled newsman ever since the girls – now women in their 40s – were in their teens.

It was a meeting he'd never even given a second thought to until the day he finally finished the book. In fact, he'd almost counted on the fact that his daughters would never ever need to know of his darkest secret.

But certainly, the manuscript changed all that. Besides being a cathartic experience, it suddenly left him with the awkward job of trying to tie up a few very important loose ends.

Of course, he knew there'd be no absolution in the process, but it was something he felt he just had to do. He didn't want either of his daughters finding out about that day near the Song Ba from someone else or have to read about it in the book.

He should have known what their reactions would be. But that didn't make it any easier.

"Dad," countered his oldest child sitting across from him as he laid out the painful story at her sister's kitchen table, "nothing you could have said or done would have really changed anything."

Except for the fact of making him feel much better 50 some years later, thought Cratty.

He also apologized to the two about the way his marriage to their mother had ended and the fact that its collapse, like the guilt he'd always carried from Viet Nam, were among the two most damnable things that he'd carry to his grave.

He suddenly realized, what an absolute selfish shit he'd been as a father as well. He now knew just what price both he and those two daughters had paid for the last 40 plus years of chasing miscreants, misfits, and misfortunes down the dark allies of his newspaper career.

And, if it hadn't been for their mother, there'd have been a couple of more casualties left on his life's battlefield.

The confession might have come as somewhat of a shock to the pair, but if it did, they certainly didn't show it. Come to think of it, Cratty took the whole thing much harder than his intimate audience.

They also seemed more than understanding about how his marriage to their mother had so tragically disintegrated.

Catrina had taken just about 12 years more than she deserved to finally conclude that her too young, dumb, and full of cum husband was a poor bet.

She filed for and received the divorce in the summer of 1980 while he was working the sports desk at an Illinois paper. Cratty lost a wife, two beautiful little girls, and a two-pack-a-day habit in one stroke.

He certainly took the whole divorce a lot harder than she did. But he found out much too late that he wasn't the center of the universe, not even his own.

Cratty consoled himself with a newfound love of running, which would soon become a lifelong addiction.

He had always possessed an addictive personality. As his first marriage came to an end, he traded cigarettes for running shoes.

Like most of his obsessions, he jumped in at the deep end. For the next decade and a half, he got into road racing, working his way up to two marathons before losing the taste for 60 and 70-mile training weeks and racing his last couple of years in Texas.

When he'd finally made his way back to Illinois and a job with a weekly chain and later Livingstone in the early 1990s, Cratty began counseling sessions. He'd started displaying some uncontrollable bouts of anger, usually over the most minor incidents.

When he first sought help at a Viet Nam Veterans Center in eastern Illinois, he was told by a qualified counselor that he exhibited classic symptoms of P.T.S.D. He was also told by the professional that it was surprising that, with his obviously addictive tendencies, he wasn't either a raging alcoholic or strung out on drugs.

The fact that he wasn't a drunk or junkie was due, according to the counselor, to his long lingering issues with his father. And it was also a pretty good explanation for the hold running had on him.

That was the first time that Cratty had been diagnosed with depression, and it was suggested that he consider prescription drugs.

But, being a newspaperman and still dependent on his creative wits, he'd refused medication.

The suggestion would surface again in the early 2000s, following a couple of angry outbursts at The Daily Call. Maybe it was the deterioration he was beginning to see in the profession that sparked the confrontations. However, regardless of the reasons, after Cratty had given up his column, he agreed to use fluoxetine, a generic form of Prozac.

Cratty just couldn't get it out of his thinning, silver-haired head; he was watching the democracy that he had loved for so long and so fervently die.

Too many of this nation's citizens were suffering under the misconception that the form of government they spent the previous 200 plus years living and thriving under was a self-perpetuating force of nature.

They had convinced themselves that it was unassailable and would always be as they once perceived it – that so-called shining city on a hill.

But they would soon learn that it was a precious commodity that required both constant vigilance and unwavering dedication. And the thing they failed to understand was that all the nuclear tipped missiles in hardened silos and submarine launch tubes, best-equipped and trained armed forces and border wall could never defend the most important commodity of all: trust in the outcome.

And while they were too busy watching the balloons, banners, rallies and attack ads of the political sideshow swirling around them, that trust had already caught the last bus out of town.

It was the profession he'd so recently abandoned that was truly the only real defense of that democracy he now watched slipping away. Without a free and unencumbered press, there was no defense against those who would stamp out the democratic fire.

That's why the profession was the only mercantile endeavor enshrined by the Founding Fathers. They knew that the form of government they were trying to construct could withstand any number of snake oil salesmen, but not a uniformed and bitterly divided populace.

The first veteran newspaperman to take Cratty under his wing was Delbert Roberts.

Del was a long-suffering, jack-of-all-trades reporter who served his entire career at LaMotte. He was also the first member of the staff Cratty was introduced to because they sat in adjoining desks in the tiny newsroom. In fact, the space was so small it seemed to recall the constant warning voiced by Sgt. Davis: "Spread out people, one ice cube would freeze the lotta ya!"

Roberts dragged the rookie by the hand and introduced him at every local government and law enforcement office in the county seat of 11,000. It was Roberts who taught Cratty the formula for writing obituaries, where the

"F.N.G." was confined for his first couple of months on the job.

While he was still in his final quarter at State University during the winter of 1970-71, Cratty started out in circulation, in charge of out of town carriers. It was there that he saw life from the business side of an old hot lead press era. And it was there where he undoubtedly picked up a bad taste in his mouth for that side of the business.

It was not unusual in those days to see silvery, molten hot lead spill out of its mold and all over a pressman's boot. When that occurred, a co-worker would have to take a carpet knife, hanging on the wall for just such occasions and cut the victim's boot off before somebody lost a foot.

But the very first newsroom lesson imparted by Roberts was the use of the number "30." Since writing in those days was done on manual typewriters, and the paper used was cut in rectangles from newsprint rolls to fit in the said typewriter, the number, usually encased in parentheses, would be needed to actually let those editing copy know when they'd reached the end of a story.

When the (30) popped up, the person editing the piece would know that they had the whole story. And stories were always done using two sheets of paper inserted in the typewriter with a carbon sheet between, ensuring that there was always a backup.

Another practice at the time, which modern computers still pay homage to, was the use of scissors and paste in a jar with a brush top. Paragraphs could be cut out and rearranged using the brush and paste. It certainly saved a lot of re-typing.

At larger papers, a double roll of typewriter width newsprint hung, usually by a wire hanger, behind the manuals with the carbon sheet already in between. That saved the constant need of placing sheets around the carbon paper every few minutes.

It also made it easier to reconstruct the first draft when pages would invariably get scrambled.

Cratty initially found it hard to break the habit of using the (30) later in his career. When VDTs and computers came on the scene, the practice, much like ubiquitous rows of constantly roaring wire machines and the youngsters who were tasked with having to constantly clear the devices, were lost to history.

It crossed Cratty's mind more than once since the winter of 2010 that lung cancer was somehow more than just a little well-deserved karma. After all, he never forgot Tuy Hoa, and it was the first thing that came to mind as the doctor pronounced what sounded to him more like a sentence than a diagnosis.

It took almost 50 years to arrive, but the God he no longer believed in seemed to be reaching out and tapping him on the shoulder.

One of the two things he dreaded most in his past had finally caught up with him. He could never ever make up for the second; the dismal outcome of his marriage to Catrina would go unpunished. And now the first – a weak and shameful moment beside a Southeast Asian rice paddy – would exact the ultimate penalty. And, as an added value for losing his faith, Cratty was at peace that there would be no retribution beyond the grave.

He wasn't above believing that his life could well be the cost of both of his shames.

But his first marriage hadn't gone completely unpunished, really. There was a punishment, a giant hole that he felt deep down inside every time he'd find himself in the company of Catrina, their children and grandkids. It was like staring at a hopelessly shattered picture frame. You could still see everyone else's image, but the spot where he was supposed to be had been ripped out, leaving a ragged gap.

Luckily, no one bothered to ask Cratty how he felt about the situation. That was probably just as well because it was very painful and even harder for him to try and explain without choking up.

Getting choked up was happening more and more since Cratty went off the mood medication during the VA counseling he'd taken up again in the summer of 2017.

The reason for the counseling was the fact that after he'd retired in late summer of 2015, Cratty had trouble convincing the government that he still had lung cancer, and that the removal of one of his lungs did not cure the disease.

The VA bureaucrats in charge of such decisions tried to tell him, because of an error in his initial filing, that he showed no signs of what they mistakenly believed were a claim of "residuals" of lung cancer. All this even though the VA oncology clinic in Indianapolis was regularly giving him CAT scans for the several clearly visible cancer spots in the one lung he still had.

The first thing his VA counselor did was take him off the fluoxetine, which had, over the years, leveled off his mood well enough, but as he had first feared, it hampered his writing.

The move probably contributed greatly to his completing the book but also led him to more profound emotional swings. He discovered that he could tear up at the simplest things, from old songs to touching movies and TV shows. He also found that he was easily distracted by memories of Viet Nam.

He would be driving down the highway and start to sing along to one of his oldie favorites and be completely unable to mouth the lyrics for the lump in his throat.

There were even times Cratty's LRRP frame of mind would creep back in the strangest situations.

Once during one of those pseudo-philosophical gab sessions that occur during lulls in newsroom banter, a youngish reporter – they were always decades younger than him – probably in an attempt at starting a joke, asked colleagues "What's the loneliest sound in the world?"

Immediately, Cratty kills the mood with the somber retort; "The loneliest sound in the world is chopper blades disappearing in the distance."

After he'd trashed the proceedings, Cratty had no interest in trying to explain to these kids that when you hear the eggbeater sound of a helicopter that has just inserted you in the bush fading off, that's the moment you know that you're completely alone.

But Cratty certainly wasn't complaining after he got off the Prozac. He liked the return to his old, normally over-reactive self. However, he was still a little embarrassed by the fact that he was a 71-year-old combat vet who was too often on the verge of tears.

Perhaps it was the chaotic nature of the political landscape that prodded him to finally complete his long efforts on the book. No matter the provocation, he completed the task.

The 2016 presidential balloting had almost sealed the plan. He found it harder and harder to scrape together anything remotely resembling love for his country, the same one he'd once been so foolishly desperate to die for. It appeared more and more like his nation of birth was reaching the end of its string and that the future, if there really was one, was quite dim.

As each day passed and the controversies and consternation grew, he started wanting to be someplace else in this world.

The final break came in two separate incidents, really, both in the winter of 2017-18. The last of the pair was an Oval Office temper tantrum in early January 2018 and the other was the re-reading of a novel he'd first come across a couple of decades earlier.

President Trump, during a discussion regarding immigration reform, reportedly referred to several predominantly black nations in the world as, in his words, "shithole countries."

Of course, once the worldwide outcry came pouring in, the Trump Administration immediately retreated behind its always not very convincing denials and increasingly embarrassing and lame counterattacks against the press and other of Trump's myriad critics.

Cratty immediately reacted with undisguised shame and lengthy Facebook rants. The rants seemed to calm some of his anger, but the shame was not as easy to dispel.

Cratty wondered if any American president, including those who founded this nation and were slaveholders themselves, had ever uttered such words inside the Oval Office. And despite knowing that some profoundly insensitive individuals had held that office over the intervening 200 plus years, he had serious doubts about that.

Obviously, more than at least a couple of avid racists have placed their asses in the desk at the heart of the somewhat ironically named White House. But one would hope that even they had the presence of mind, political good sense or simply the common decency to avoid this kind of blasphemy.

They well might have harbored the thought, but they had enough respect for the office and country to bite their lip.

Then it also occurred to Cratty that this poor excuse of a so-called man, occupying the highest office in the land, was a perfect representative of everything that churned within him and was the very embodiment of the point he'd been trying to make in the pages of a book for the last two decades.

Here was a narcissistic, sanity-challenged, and barely literate human being, who despite a history marked by vile word and deed, rode his hatred for the truth and those who seek it to the presidency of a people he neither respected nor understood anymore. He is clearly without the knowledge of or interest in any of the values that America once stood for.

About two years into his retirement, while Cratty was in the process of finishing his own work, he re-read a book he'd first come across almost 20 years earlier. *The Sorrow of War: A Novel of North Vietnam* was penned by Bao Ninh, an NVA combat veteran of the Southeast Asian conflict.

The author fought against the South Vietnamese and Americans for seven years. There were no breaks in his military service, not so much as a weekend pass. Ninh left his home in downtown Hanoi when he was just a couple of years younger than Cratty in 1968 and didn't return until the war had ended in 1975.

Perhaps they could have faced off across a battlefield in the South's Central Highlands. But as luck would have it, there was two to three years' difference in tours.

The last year of Ninh's service was spent unearthing, logging and re-burying thousands upon thousands of NVA dead. He himself had been one of just five members of an NVA battalion (close to 500 men) to survive the war.

The communists and their Southern antagonists suffered terribly over the course of the fight with and against the U.S. And Cratty couldn't even begin to imagine the overwhelming hole in generations the struggle must have left behind on both sides of Vietnamese society. It was a civil war that, like most such conflicts, maims, and destroys millions of victims, inflicting untold devastation that may never heal.

The Viet Cong and their NVA cohorts were the victims of the most horrific and advanced weaponry that money could buy. America's billions upon billions of dollars lavished upon this country's "military/industrial complex" resulted in casualty rates that few nations have ever experienced. And the VC and NVA had no air force, effective navy or real artillery much beyond mortars to cope with the onslaught.

Illustrating the point were the words of a North Vietnamese diplomat who once explained: "You Americans will kill 10 of us to every one of you, but the day will come when you will grow tired and go home."

The thing that seemed to resonate most for Cratty in Ninh's book was the struggle from the NVA veteran's point of view. Even though his side was victorious, you couldn't tell it from his account. In fact, there seemed very little if any joy in his re-telling of the story.

It only took a few paragraphs of his tale to understand that Cratty had much more in common with Ninh than he now had with many of his own countrymen.

According to Ninh, there were no winners in that or any other war. The same casualties of body, mind, and spirit haunt both the victors and the losers, especially at the battlefield or "grunt" level. Political causes and elites may enjoy some brief form of exhilaration and accomplishment in winning such struggles, but this satisfaction is not visited on the actual combatants.

After finishing the Vietnamese veteran's account, Cratty had discovered a kindred spirit. Another with the same scars both emotional and physical, who was indeed a member of a much wider brotherhood that expanded to both sides of the battlefield. Ninh, like Cratty, had found himself almost alone and wanting in a strange land.

In fact, Ninh's book was initially banned in Viet Nam, his government refusing to accept any view of the conflict other than as a glorious and uplifting struggle. For the first decade after publication, Vietnamese who wanted to read his book had to do so with poorly reproduced, pirated copies.

Despite being banned in his homeland, the novel enjoyed widespread acceptance across the globe.

A very telling point in the book and most likely one of the chief reasons for it being banned in Viet Nam, was Ninh's exposure of the fact that quite a few of his nation's political elite – Communist Party hierarchy and leading government officials – managed to spirit their own children out of the country to European colleges to avoid military service during those years.

That must have been the Vietnamese equivalent of having your father's doctor write you a letter about phantom bone spurs to avoid having to serve.

Ninh's novel indeed spoke to Cratty and seemed to help lift some small part of his psychological burden. And the more he thought about it, Cratty was coming to a life-changing decision.

He had once considered finding a lawn chair and a shaded stretch of highway to sit and watch the cars go by.

Life had made a complete turn for Cratty. He had gone from a career he once saw as not only promising but successful, to an old man trapped in both his accomplishments and sins, trying desperately to find something worth saving in all the fucking mess.

He had more than enough to be proud of, from two fabulous daughters, four spectacular grandchildren, finally a wife he really loved and a newspaper career that did make more than just a little mark on a host of places.

But a quiet seat beside a road kept calling.

And then, as if his initial introduction to Agent Orange wasn't enough to question his already fading patriotism, early in 2018 – more than seven years from his lung cancer sentence – the VA informed Cratty they had discovered a growth on his larynx. Any patriotic feelings that might have survived were now completely dashed.

Then, out of the blue came a brief flash, a picture scrolling by on a Viet Nam veterans' Facebook page.

A fully outfitted veteran carved in stone, web gear and shouldered M-16 was marching resolutely into a solid block of granite as if to try and catch up with fellow ghosts on the Viet Nam War Memorial.

It was a perfect representation of how Cratty and probably thousands upon thousands of other Agent Orange sufferers must now see themselves. Those slowly but most certainly succumbing to the fatal wounds of the very same conflict that had already claimed more than 58,000 of their comrades on the now silent battlefields of Viet Nam. And this statue – in a park in Rochester, N.Y. – was a fitting depiction of those still lingering casualties who were now left with nothing but a final date to join the dead.

And the more he thought about it, Cratty came to the realization that those who died outright in 'Nam might have been luckier than those like himself who were still waiting to expire.

Those names carved in the Viet Nam Memorial Wall's black expanse didn't live to see what the nation they paid the ultimate sacrifice for had become.

After the second cancer diagnosis, Cratty believed he'd found just the highway to sit beside and as luck would have it, he probably wouldn't need that lawn chair.

As he remembered it, there was probably any number of kilometer markers available along Viet Nam's aptly named "Street Without Joy" – Highway 1.

He couldn't quite make the same spectacle of himself as a naked old lady, but he could probably cause the same quizzical looks from a people he might now have found he had a lot more in common with than his current society.

Cratty suddenly felt that the future he saw waning in his own homeland was now vibrant in a nation where he'd spent the most meaningful year of his life.

He might end up being subjected to a form of government he'd been taught since birth was the very heart of darkness: communism. Cratty suddenly saw the differences as almost negligible. In fact, after coming across Ninh's remembrances, he was discovering he had a lot more in common with his former enemies than he once thought.

He might also, in the way of making some small amends, be of some help to the thousands of Vietnamese afflicted with many of the same ailments visited upon them by the same people and chemicals as himself.

He now wore a black bracelet and sported a window sticker that offered: "NOT EVERYONE WHO LOST HIS LIFE IN VIET NAM DIED THERE. AND NOT EVERYONE WHO RETURNED FROM VIET NAM EVER LEFT THERE."

It seemed almost the ultimate karma for Cratty to end his life in the very place where he lost it and certainly, emotionally at least, never left.

(30)